IRAQ
AND THE FALL OF
SADDAM HUSSEIN

Jason Richie

The Oliver Press, Inc.
Minneapolis

The Oliver Press, Inc.
Charlotte Square
5707 West 36th Street
Minneapolis, MN 55416-2510

Library of Congress Cataloging-in-Publication Data

Richie, Jason, 1966-
     Iraq and the fall of Saddam Hussein / Jason Richie.
          p. cm.
     Summary: Examines Saddam Hussein's rise to power in Iraq and
discusses the Iran-Iraq War, the Persian Gulf War, the United Nations'
efforts to disarm Iraq, and Operation Iraqi Freedom.
     Includes bibliographical references and index.
     ISBN 1-881508-63-3 (lib. bdg.) : $24.95
          1. Persian Gulf War, 1991—Juvenile literature. 2. Iraq War, 2003—
Juvenile Literature. [1. Persian Gulf War, 1991. 2. Iraq War, 2003.
3. Hussein, Saddam, 1937-. 4. Iraq—Politics and government—1991-.]
     I. Title.

DS79.723.R53 2003
956.7044—dc21

                                        2003049861

ISBN 1-881508-63-3
Printed in the United States of America

09 08 07 06 05 04   8 7 6 5 4 3 2

Contents

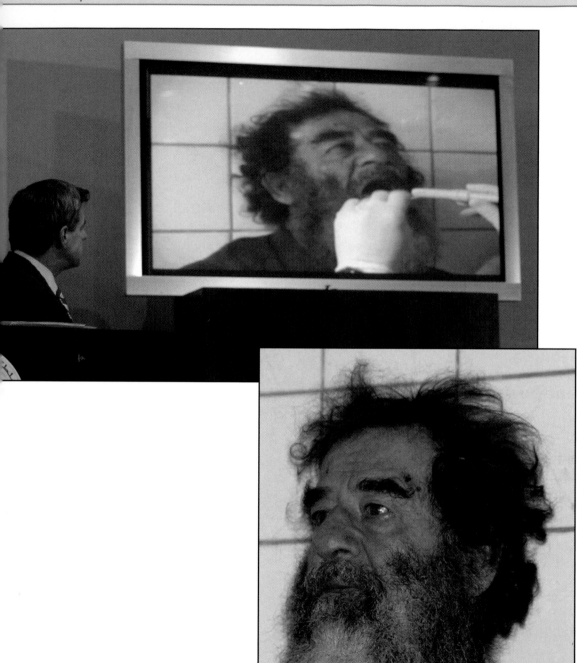

INTRODUCTION

"We Got Him."
December 2003

On April 9, 2003, hundreds of jubilant Iraqis, aided by U.S. Marines, toppled a giant statue of Saddam Hussein in downtown Baghdad, Iraq. A coalition of nations led by the United States and Great Britain had overrun the country in a three-week war, driving Saddam from power. But many Iraqis did not feel truly free until December 13, when, after months of searching, U.S. forces captured Saddam at a farm 10 miles south of his hometown of Tikrit. Like his statue, the man had fallen far. Saddam was found hiding in a hole in the ground, and he surrendered without firing a shot.

The war for Iraq did not end with the fall of Baghdad in April, however, nor with the capture of Saddam Hussein eight months later. Iraq is a diverse country of 25 million people. There are Arabs, Kurds, Turks, Assyrians, and others; Sunni Muslims, Shi'ah Muslims, and Christians; those who favor rule by one person (autocracy), rule by the people (democracy), or rule by religious authority (theocracy). All the groups want some power, some want all. They will battle for Iraq in the years to come.

The fighting did not begin with Saddam, either. After losing World War I (1914-1918), the Ottoman Empire was dismantled and most of its territory claimed by Great Britain and the other victorious countries. In 1921, the British created Iraq from parts of these lands. The country has been at war ever since as people have fought and killed for their vision of Iraq's future.

U.S. ambassador to Iraq Paul Bremer showed a videotape of the captured Saddam Hussein to the press on December 14, 2003. Iraqis in the audience cheered when Bremer announced, "Ladies and gentlemen, we got him." Saddam was dirty and unshaven after his months of running and hiding.

Some wanted Iraq to serve Great Britain, which installed the first of three Iraqi kings. Others hated the British and wanted to unite all Arabs into a single nation. Still others wanted Iraq to be for the Iraqis and not part of some larger Arab whole. The pro-British monarchy was overthrown in 1958, and coup followed coup until 1979, when Saddam Hussein assumed absolute power.

Saddam killed and maimed more than one million people over the next two dozen years in a ruthless quest to rule Iraq and make it the leading power in the Middle East. Many of the Iraqis who perished were the victims of political murders, massacres of rebellious villagers, and acts of torture. Others were soldiers who died in wars that Saddam started with Iran and Kuwait. The second of these conflicts led to the Persian Gulf War in 1991.

Following the war, Kurds in the north and Shi'ah in the south rebelled. Each group hoped to break free of the murderous dictator and give form to its own vision of Iraq. But Saddam crushed the rebels, killing 80,000 and forcing millions to flee. Over the next decade, he waged war for the soul of the country like never before. The front page of every newspaper was filled with pictures of Saddam and articles praising Saddam. The people were forced to proclaim their love for their leader at mass rallies.

But individual Iraqis fought back, like Farris Salman, who spoke out against Saddam. Thugs known as the Fedayeen Saddam—"Saddam's men of sacrifice"—came for Salman one afternoon in early March 2003. They grabbed him by the arms. He was given a choice between instant death and having his tongue cut out. He wanted to live, so he opened his mouth. The Fedayeen grabbed his tongue with pliers and cut it off with a box cutter. It was a stiff price to pay for cursing Saddam Hussein, but at least Salman survived.

Another resister, Kadhim Sabbit al-Datajji, spent eight years in an Iraqi prison for refusing to join Saddam's Baath Party. By the time of his release in October 2002, he had lost count of the tortures he suffered. Guards beat him with heavy sticks, shocked him with electricity, and even pulled out his toenails. "Of course you scream," he told the *New York Times*, "but it is normal to scream."

The U.S. and Great Britain fought for Iraq, too. In the 1980s, Saddam had spent lavishly to develop chemical, biological, and nuclear weapons—called weapons of mass destruction for their ability to kill large numbers of people in a single attack. That was not the kind of Iraq the two Western powers wanted to see in the middle of the richest oil-producing region in the world. Following the Persian Gulf War, the United Nations (UN) demanded Saddam's disarmament and sent inspectors to Iraq to ensure its compliance. The inspectors destroyed some of Saddam's weapons, but a number remained unaccounted for.

After terrorists attacked the U.S. on September 11, 2001, killing thousands, the missing Iraqi weapons took on renewed significance. President George W. Bush feared another terrorist attack, possibly with these weapons. He declared his intention to disarm Iraq. Saddam failed to account for the missing weapons. So on March 20, 2003, a coalition led by American and British troops invaded Iraq and drove Saddam and the Baath Party from power in less than a month.

It was a controversial war, not sanctioned by the UN's ruling Security Council as the first Gulf War had been. The controversy continued as no evidence of weapons of mass destruction was found after months of searching. When Bush appealed to the UN in September 2003 to take on a bigger role in Iraq and to "all nations of goodwill" to provide help to rebuild Iraq, he received no immediate pledges of aid. The president remained committed, however, stating that the coalition was "helping to improve the daily lives of the Iraqi people."

One of those improvements was that in December 2003 Saddam Hussein was imprisoned at a secret location awaiting a trial by his own people. Iraqis were now free to pursue their own visions for the future of their country.

CHAPTER I
The Rise of Saddam Hussein al-Tikriti 1921-1989

In Iraq, the name Saddam means "one who confronts." When Subha Talfah picked the name for her newborn boy on April 28, 1937, she chose perfectly. Hussein, the infant's middle name, came from his father, Hussein al-Majid. Saddam Hussein means literally "Saddam, son of Hussein." It is an Iraqi tradition for men to take the name of their birthplace as their last name. Later in life, Saddam officially changed his hometown to Tikrit, making his full name Saddam Hussein al-Tikriti. The proper short form is Saddam.

Saddam was not born in Tikrit, but a few miles away in the smaller peasant village of Al-Ouja. Tikrit was more famous, though. It was the birthplace of Saladin, the Muslim general who captured Jerusalem from the Christian crusaders in 1187. The adult Saddam would see himself as a modern-day Saladin, destined to repeat the famous general's conquest.

Hussein al-Majid either abandoned his family a few years after Saddam's birth, or died; both versions are told. The greatest influence on young Saddam became Subha's brother, Khairallah Talfah. Saddam worshiped his Uncle Khairallah. During World War II (1939-1945), Khairallah worshiped Adolf Hitler. One of Hitler's finest qualities, he felt, was his racism—his fanatical belief that Germans were superior to other peoples. Khairallah was an extremist like this, too, but he believed Arabs

Saddam Hussein (below) spoke to his troops before sending them to war against Iran in 1980. Saddam compared himself to Saladin (1138-1193, top), the Muslim hero who recaptured the city of Jerusalem from Christian crusaders.

were the superior race. Many years later, after Saddam took over Iraq, Khairallah published a pamphlet called "Three Whom God Should Not Have Created: Persians, Jews, and Flies."

Khairallah saved his greatest contempt for Westerners, especially the British. Like most Iraqis, he saw them as back-stabbing imperialists interested only in exploiting Iraq's location and oil. In 1941, Khairallah joined a pro-Nazi conspiracy to bomb a British air base outside Baghdad. The plan miscarried, and Khairallah was imprisoned for the next five years.

Creation of a Nation

Iraq's problems with Great Britain stretched back to World War I (1914-1918). Before and during the war, the Turkish Ottoman Empire ruled the Middle East. There were no separate nations. The Ottoman Turks were allies of the Germans and Austrians. When the British won the war, they occupied much of the Turks' empire; the French occupied other parts. What remained is modern-day Turkey.

In 1921, Great Britain created Iraq from lands under its control. The new boundaries set by the British forced three distinct groups—Shi'ah Muslims, Sunni Muslims, and Kurds—to join together in one country, even though these people did not get along. The majority of Muslims adhere to the Sunni branch of Islam; central Iraq, including Baghdad, is home to many Sunnis. Shi'ah (also called Shiite) Muslims have a different interpretation of Islam. They are a minority in the Middle East, but they are the majority (about 60 percent) in Iraq, living mainly in the south. Kurds represent about 20 percent of the population and live in the north. Although most Kurds are Sunni, they are a different ethnic group than other Iraqis, who are Arabs.

After creating this new nation, the British installed a weak leader, King Faisal I, and controlled him with their powerful military. The Iraqis were furious. They had been promised full independence for helping the British overthrow the Turks. The British had their reasons for changing their minds, however.

Before the start of World War I, the extensive Ottoman Empire included Turkey, Iraq, Israel, Lebanon, and portions of Jordan, Syria, Saudi Arabia, and Yemen.

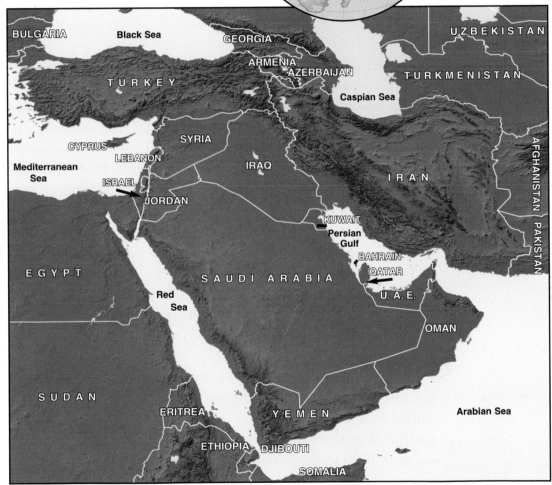

They suspected the area had oil. (It did, as they discovered in 1927.) Also, control of Iraq gave Great Britain a land route to the Persian Gulf, which was on the way to British India.

The Iraqis hated King Faisal from the beginning. Over the next 37 years, only one of Faisal's successors enjoyed any popular support. After World War II ended in 1945, Khairallah Talfah was released from prison and began working to overthrow the monarchy. As Saddam Hussein grew to adulthood in the 1950s, he became involved, too. By then Great Britain had weakened. It barely survived the fight with Hitler. After the war, the British Empire slowly collapsed. A vacuum of power developed in the Middle East by the late 1940s.

Three forces rushed to fill the void: the Soviet Union, the United States, and the Arabs themselves. Soviet Russia hoped to gain allies and block Western access to oil. The United States opposed the Russians' aims, especially their drive for oil. In 1940, the United States produced 70 percent of the world's oil. The Middle East accounted for 5 percent. By 1955, however, Middle East oil production had jumped to 20 percent, while the U.S. share had dipped to 43 percent. Clearly, if the West hoped to remain prosperous, it needed access to Middle East oil. To keep the oil flowing, the U.S. pumped foreign aid into the region. In January 1957, President Dwight Eisenhower even threatened to use military force to counter any aggression in the region by the Soviets or their Arab allies. By the late 1950s, it was clear that the U.S. considered the Middle East vital to its national security.

The third force to fill the void left by the weakening British was the Arabs themselves. Many were Arab nationalists, who wanted to unite all Arabs into a single nation free of all foreign control—Western and Soviet. Others wanted strong independent nations. Even those who preferred separate countries, however, wanted Arabs in control and foreigners out.

One area almost all Arabs agreed on was Israel. The United States and Great Britain had strongly influenced the creation of the Jewish state in May 1948. In addition to having religious differences with the Jews, Arab leaders bitterly opposed the creation of Israel from territory they considered theirs. They immediately launched a war to destroy it. Their effort failed, but they continued to plot Israel's destruction. To many Arabs, Israel was a symbol of Western, especially American, dominance.

Saddam's Early Years in Politics

These events formed the backdrop of Saddam's early life. He grew up on the streets, using his fists to settle accounts. In 1957, he joined the Arab-nationalist Baath Party. From the beginning he was an especially violent member. Saddam killed for the first time in 1958, murdering a communist who ran afoul of Uncle Khairallah. The same year, King Faisal II was assassinated by the military. His successor, General Abdul Karim Qasim (sometimes spelled Kassem), was a disappointment whom the Baathists attempted to assassinate in October 1959. Saddam was one of seven hit men. The plan failed and Saddam was shot in the leg. He escaped and spent the next three and a half years in exile in Syria and Egypt.

The Baathists and other parties finally murdered Qasim in February 1963. Saddam missed the bloody coup, or takeover, but he hurried back to Baghdad to help eliminate the general's followers. Beatings, killings, and torture were common. Saddam himself supervised interrogations as a member of the Baath intelligence committee. Saddam's knack for violence made him invaluable to party leaders, who needed a talented thug to do their dirty work. The mastermind of the 1963 coup was General Ahmad Hassan al-Bakr. He picked Saddam for his bodyguard and right-hand man.

In November 1963, the Baathists were tossed from the government by the other parties involved in the coup. During the five years that the Baathists remained out of power, Saddam built the party's internal security apparatus, using the fiendish methods of Joseph Stalin as a model. As dictator of the Soviet

General Abdul Karim Qasim (1914-1963) dead in his chair after being murdered by Baathists

Union from the early 1920s to his death in 1953, Stalin had created the world's most brutal and repressive police state. When al-Bakr and the Baath Party finally gained control of the government in July 1968, al-Bakr appointed Saddam head of national security. With al-Bakr's approval, Saddam worked to become the most feared man in Iraq.

By 1970, al-Bakr had elevated his talented protégé to vice president. Over the next 10 years, Saddam rounded up and eliminated (by torture, assassination, or exile) anyone who threatened his or al-Bakr's power. He typically accused victims of plotting to overthrow the government, usually with help from Jewish or American agents. The government, the military, the general population—eventually the ruthless Saddam cowed them all. One detainee remembers Saddam personally throwing a torture victim—still alive—into a bathtub full of acid. Such stories circulated and, true or not, convinced the public not to challenge Saddam or the Baath Party.

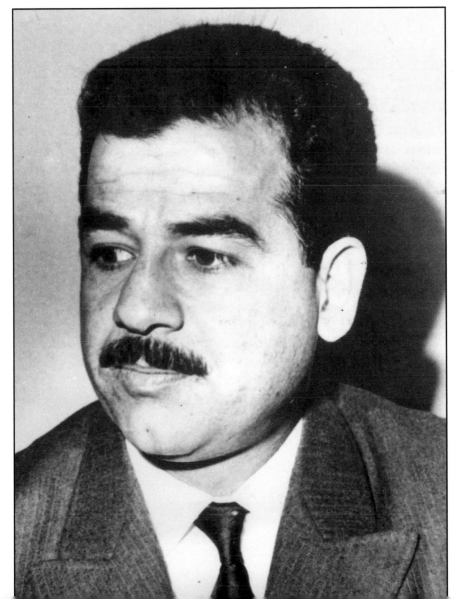

Saddam Hussein in 1970, when he was vice president of Iraq and head of national security

The Power of Oil

While running the country as al-Bakr's deputy, Saddam built an impressive record of reform and modernization. His greatest reform was nationalizing Iraq's oil industry. Until June 1972, Iraq did not control its own oil. The Americans, British, Dutch, and French did. The Westerners controlled production because they controlled the market. In other words, when the Iraqis tried drilling and selling their own oil, they suddenly found no buyers for the product. Saddam changed all this. First he allied Iraq with the Soviets in return for their promise to buy Iraqi-produced oil. Then, to split the Western oil coalition, he offered cheap oil to France and permitted its oil company to continue to develop Iraq's oil fields. France backed out of its agreement with the other countries, the West's ability to monopolize the market dissolved, and Iraq took charge of its own oil fields.

With the world's second largest oil reserves to draw from, Iraq was awash in revenue. It built new schools, hospitals, a national radio and television network, and huge factories packed with the latest production equipment. Rural villages were wired for electricity, and farmers received modern machinery. A network of pipelines was laid to transport oil from fields and refineries to ports. New technology was imported to solve countless other problems.

Arming Iraq

Oil bought weapons, too. Iraq's military budget increased ten times between 1970 and 1975. Saddam's first cousin, Adnan Khairallah, became minister of defense in 1977, and the two of them basically controlled the military and its spending. Saddam bought arms mostly from the Soviet Union and France, but several other Western nations were also suppliers. Tanks, armored personnel carriers, trucks, artillery, helicopters, fighter jets, missiles, machine guns, rifles—you name it, the Russians and the West were eager to sell it.

Saddam did not stop with conventional arms. He built stockpiles of biological and chemical agents that he could use as weapons of mass destruction. To create highly infectious bacteria like anthrax, Saddam turned once again to France. The French signed on to build Iraq's first bacteria lab in 1974. They apparently accepted Saddam's explanation that the lab would produce animal vaccines. Perhaps it did, but it produced anthrax, too. When inhaled, anthrax causes lesions in the lungs and brain and is usually fatal. Besides producing anthrax, Saddam used the lab and others like it to make botulinum, a neurotoxin ("nerve poison") that paralyses the respiratory muscles to cause suffocation. Other biological agents Iraq produced included cholera and typhoid. Cholera causes severe vomiting and diarrhea, killing by dehydration. Typhoid is an often fatal intestinal disease.

Saddam also ordered chemical agents to be developed, including mustard gas, sarin, and VX. Mustard gas causes huge blisters on human tissue. If it is inhaled, blisters form inside the lungs, which then fill with fluid, causing the victim to suffocate. Sarin and VX are nerve agents that shut down the nervous system. One drop of sarin will kill a person, and VX is even more potent. What makes agents like sarin and VX so terrifying is that they can be produced in "dual-use" facilities that also manufacture common fertilizers. As with his production of anthrax, Saddam told the world he was building a plant for constructive good. He then used it to make millions of pounds of these deadly chemicals.

Ultimately, Saddam desired nuclear weapons. Armed with them, he believed he could dominate the Arab world, confront and even destroy Israel, and remove the West from the Middle East for good. Saddam had to be sneaky to build his bomb, though. Iraq had signed the Nuclear Non-Proliferation Treaty in 1968. That meant inspectors from the International Atomic Energy Agency (IAEA) occasionally checked to ensure no nuclear weapons were being built. (They did the same in all nations that signed the non-proliferation treaty.) The inspectors proved no match for the clever Saddam. While Iraq pumped billions of dollars into its nuclear weapons program, the inspectors time and again proclaimed it nuclear-free.

For help with its nuclear project, Iraq turned once again to the Soviet Union and France. The Russians built, and later upgraded, Iraq's first nuclear reactor. They also trained more than 100 Iraqi nuclear physicists. When they declined to provide further support in 1975, Saddam made a deal with Prime Minister Jacques Chirac of France. In exchange for cheap oil and several big construction contracts, Chirac sold Iraq a nuclear reactor capable of producing plutonium for nuclear bombs. France also agreed to train another 600 Iraqi nuclear physicists. The deal was worth billions of dollars to the French. In 1981, attack jets from Israel destroyed Iraq's nuclear reactor. Saddam just started over. He still had the will to develop nuclear weapons and the scientists to do it.

The New President Goes to War

Saddam overthrew Ahmad Hassan al-Bakr in July 1979 to become president and supreme leader of Iraq. Just six months earlier, Shi'ah religious leader Ayatollah Ruhollah Khomeini had seized power in neighboring Iran, instituting a fundamentalist Islamic republic. This was a major blow to the United States. For more than 30 years, Iran had been ruled by the pro-American shah, Muhammad Reza Shah Pahlevi. U.S. leaders counted on the shah to be a stabilizing and anticommunist force in the region and had armed Iran with the latest military hardware. When the shah fell to the fanatically anti-American Khomeini in January 1979, the U.S. lost a key Middle East ally. Adding insult to injury, Iranians stormed the U.S. embassy in their capital of Tehran and took 52 Americans hostage. Saddam saw the situation as a big opportunity for himself.

Saddam hated, feared, and desired Iran all at the same time. Under the shah, Iran's made-in-America military had checked

Saddam's ambition to dominate the Middle East. That was the hate part. The fear involved Khomeini, who had lived in exile in Iraq for many years and was now actively inciting Shi'ah Iraqis to rise up and overthrow Saddam. The desire was all about oil, which Iran had lots of. Saddam's solution to all three problems was force. He would invade Iran, destroy Khomeini, and take the oil.

Ayatollah Ruhollah Khomeini (1900-1989) pictured in 1978 in France during his exile

The United States would later point to Iraq's invasion of Iran as proof that Saddam was a grave danger to peace in the Middle East. What the Americans never mentioned, however, was the evidence that suggested they gave Saddam the green light to invade. In July 1980, it appears that top officials from the United States and Iraq met to discuss ways to contain volatile Iran. America could not openly support Iraq or its invasion of Iran because Saddam supported Palestinian terrorism against Israel. Still, a successful Iraqi invasion of Iran would be helpful if it neutralized Khomeini's Islamic extremism. Saddam was seen as an enforcer of the "Carter Doctrine." Earlier in the

President Jimmy Carter (left) met with the shah of Iran, a longtime friend of the U.S., in 1977. The shah ruled from 1941 to 1979, except for a brief period during the 1950s, when nationalists took over and forced him to flee Iran.

year, U.S. president Jimmy Carter had warned that he would use "any means necessary" to ensure that no power hostile to the United States gained control of the Middle East.

Even if the U.S. never approved Saddam's invasion of Iran before it took place in September 1980, the Americans certainly aided Iraq afterward. Once Ronald Reagan became president in 1981, the U.S. shared with Saddam a steady stream of satellite photos detailing Iranian troop locations. It also sold Iraq helicopters that could be (and were) converted to military use. Reagan sent Donald Rumsfeld as a special representative to Baghdad to rally Western support for the war. The U.S. even helped build Saddam's stockpile of banned weapons. High-technology equipment first sold to Iraq in 1985 was later used to build weapons of mass destruction. Finally, when Saddam used his chemical weapons against Iranian troops and cities, the Americans did little to stop him beyond halfhearted protests.

By the end of the eight-year Iran-Iraq War, Iraq had used chemical-filled bombs, rockets, and artillery shells to kill or injure some 50,000 Iranians in close to 200 attacks. Saddam also dumped poison gas on his own people—Kurds in northern Iraq seeking independence who had allied themselves with Iran. In just one attack in March 1988, Saddam's forces used chemical weapons to wipe out 5,000 Kurds in the town of Halabja. About 100,000 Kurds died during Saddam's retaliation against them in 1988.

After the Iran-Iraq War

In the end, Iraq defeated Iran—but just barely. Iran accepted a cease-fire in August 1988. Neither country had gained any territory or resolved any issues. Casualty figures can only be estimated, but probably one million people died, thousands more were wounded, and millions became refugees. Saddam survived, and Iraq's military emerged from the war as the second strongest in the Middle East (behind only Israel) and fourth largest in the world. Saddam's stockpile of chemical weapons

Poison gas victims lie dead in the Kurdish village of Halabja in northern Iraq.

was greatly enlarged, and he now knew how to use it. The murderous war put Saddam on the defensive in his own country, however, as 200,000 Iraqis had been killed to gain this armed might and perhaps another 500,000 injured. About 70,000 Iraqi soldiers were prisoners of war.

Saddam was also deeply in debt. He owed tens of billions of dollars to the West and to Arab neighbors. His nation was in shambles and required hundreds of billions of dollars to rebuild. Iraq was spending more than twice as much money as it earned from oil (practically Iraq's only income). It was clear Saddam needed a quick infusion of money, and the best source of cash in the Middle East was oil. He began to look around for answers. He settled his gaze southward, to the fabulously rich oil fields of Kuwait and Saudi Arabia.

Iranian soldiers carry coffins of their comrades killed during the Iran-Iraq War. This exchange of remains in 2002 was one of many between the two countries.

CHAPTER 2

The Persian Gulf War
1990-1991

On December 27, 1979, the Soviet Union invaded Afghanistan. The aggression shocked the United States. Afghanistan was on the eastern fringes of the Middle East, where America bought much of its oil. President Jimmy Carter responded on January 23, 1980, with this warning, which became known as the Carter Doctrine: "An attempt by any outside force to gain control of the Persian Gulf region will be regarded as an assault on the vital interests of the United States of America, and such an assault will be repelled by any means necessary, including military force."

When Saddam Hussein invaded Kuwait on August 2, 1990, President George H. W. Bush and his advisors thought of the Carter Doctrine. Iraq itself sat on about 11 percent of the world's known supply of oil. With the addition of Kuwait, that percentage jumped to 20. It was bad enough for one person to control so much oil, but the real fear was that Iraq would continue south and take the oil fields of Saudi Arabia. Saddam's share of the world's oil would then stand at around 46 percent. He could manipulate the price of oil and thus the global economy. Even if he did nothing to restrict the flow of cheap oil, Saddam would have increased oil revenue to fuel his known programs of building weapons of mass destruction and supporting terrorism. Bush vowed to meet the threat, with military force if needed.

On January 15, 1991, President George H. W. Bush met with his close advisers to discuss the possibility of war with Iraq.

Saddam's invasion surprised Bush and his senior advisers. Until the day he invaded Kuwait, Saddam was not considered a serious threat to the United States. In fact, America supported Iraq in its war with Iran from 1980 to 1988. Saddam's move to control the Persian Gulf oil supply, however, was unacceptable.

Buildup to War

The first evidence of trouble came on July 17, 1990, when satellite photos showed Iraqi military equipment being positioned near the Kuwaiti border. Included were several hundred T-72 tanks, Iraq's best, which Saddam had purchased from the Soviet Union. General Colin Powell, chairman of the Joint Chiefs of Staff and America's top military leader, was not overly concerned when he saw the photos, however. Key equipment needed to invade, like artillery and fuel trucks, was missing. Powell dismissed the movement as a practice exercise, or a bluff to scare the Kuwaitis. At that moment, Saddam was pressing Kuwait to lower its oil production so that world oil prices would remain high.

Saddam was also disputing Kuwait's ownership of two islands that blocked Iraq's access to the Persian Gulf. In addition, there was a disputed oil field that straddled the Iraq-Kuwait border. The Iran-Iraq War had drained Saddam's treasury, and he needed that oil field and access to the Gulf. He hatched a plan to take the islands and the oil field by force. On July 25, he met with U.S. ambassador April Glaspie in Baghdad and tried to learn if the U.S. would block a partial invasion of Kuwait. Glaspie and leaders in Washington were aware of Saddam's plight. They were willing to let Saddam have the islands and the oil field. Glaspie hinted as much when she assured Saddam that Bush had "no opinion on the Arab-Arab conflicts like your border disagreement with Kuwait." Saddam's great blunder was that sometime during the next week, he decided to take all of Kuwait.

At around the same time, Powell was reassured by Middle East leaders that Saddam would not invade Kuwait. This was no trick on their part. Saddam had given them his word the movement was a practice exercise. The stage was set for a terrible surprise.

Additional satellite images received on August 1 convinced Powell that Saddam was indeed launching an invasion. The tanks were speeding into battle formation; the fuel trucks had appeared; artillery, helicopters, and fighter jets were moving in. Powell suggested to Defense Secretary Dick Cheney that Bush warn Saddam not to invade. Cheney still thought Iraq was bluffing. He never asked the White House to issue the warning. That night, Iraq invaded Kuwait with 120,000 soldiers and almost 1,000 tanks.

The Bush team quickly realized that Saddam did not have to stop with Kuwait. To the south beckoned the oil-rich fields of Saudi Arabia, with only a fraction of the Saudi army blocking the way. Indeed, satellite photos showed Iraqi forces moving in that direction. Bush decided to defend Saudi Arabia and, if necessary, to use armed force to evict Iraq from Kuwait. To defend the Saudis, the United States began moving its first forces into the area on August 7 as part of Operation Desert Shield. At the same time, Bush and Secretary of State James Baker began building a coalition (a group allied for a common cause) of more than 30 United Nations (UN) member countries to force Saddam to give up Kuwait.

As coalition military units poured into the Middle East over the next few months, economic sanctions (penalties imposed on countries violating international law) were put into place by the UN Security Council to force Iraq's retreat. This did nothing, however, to budge Saddam. On November 29, 1990, the Security Council passed Resolution 678. The resolution gave Iraq until January 15, 1991, to leave Kuwait or face war with the coalition.

Saddam was convinced he could outlast the coalition. He believed his Arab neighbors would eventually bail out of the U.S.-led effort, causing its collapse. Saddam also did not think

U.S. airpower would destroy his army. After what he assumed would be a few days of bombardment, he would launch his ground forces into what he proclaimed would be the "mother of all battles." Saddam did not hope to win the ground war against the coalition. He did, however, expect to inflict thousands of casualties. The Iranians had suffered 375,000 casualties fighting Iraq in the 1980s. Saddam saw no reason why his army, which performed well during the invasion of Kuwait, could not repeat the performance. Thousands of dead and injured would demoralize coalition leaders and convince them to negotiate an end to the war.

By January 1991, Saddam Hussein had moved more than half of Iraq's total combat force into Kuwait: about 550,000 men, more than 3,500 tanks, around 3,000 armored personnel carriers, and almost 2,500 pieces of artillery. Iraq had a large, modernized air force, with 750 combat aircraft. From bases in Iraq, these planes were capable of flying up to 1,000 missions ("sorties") per day against the coalition. To shoot down the enemy, Iraq fielded a powerful surface-to-air missile system and more than 7,500 antiaircraft guns. U.S. intelligence believed Saddam also had up to 150 Scud ballistic missiles armed with deadly chemicals such as VX and mustard gas. It was possible that Iraq also had enough of another deadly nerve agent, sarin, to load into as many as 20,000 artillery shells or up to 4,500 aerial bombs.

United against Saddam were 540,000 soldiers from more than 30 nations. Countries of all sizes were involved in the coalition, including larger nations such as the United States, France, and Britain, as well as smaller countries like Oman, Belgium, and Honduras. There were also nations that did not provide troops but contributed in other ways, such as sending money, supplies, and medical personnel and equipment. Coalition airpower included more than 1,700 combat aircraft from 12 countries, although most of the planes were American. Sixty B-52 Stratofortress bombers from the U.S. Air Force

Two of the planes the U.S. was prepared to contribute to a war against Iraq. Above, a B-52 bomber awaits mission instructions, armed with M-117 150-pound bombs. At right, with a wingspan that stretches over half the length of a football field (185 feet), the B-52G Stratofortress bomber is an impressive sight at takeoff.

stood ready at bases as far away as the United States. Stationed in the Persian Gulf and Red Sea were six U.S. Navy aircraft carriers and their support ships, two battleships, and several submarines. The coalition land force included about 2,200 of the most advanced tanks in the world, including 1,900 M1A1 Abrams from the United States. While the Iraqis fielded more tanks, fewer than 1,000 were top-notch T-72s.

Operation Desert Storm, the campaign to dislodge Iraq from Kuwait, would unfold in four phases. The first would be an air campaign against targets inside Iraq. Air strikes and submarine-launched cruise missiles would hit power plants, oil refineries, airfields and aircraft, telecommunications systems, air defense systems, weapons factories, railroads, and bridges—anything that contributed to Saddam's ability to make war. In phase two, the air campaign would shift focus to Iraqi air forces and air defense systems in Kuwait. The elimination of these would free coalition jets and bombers to begin the third phase, bombing the Iraqi ground forces in Kuwait. Then, after the enemy was "softened," the final, decisive ground-attack phase would begin.

War in the Skies

The UN deadline for Saddam's troops to leave Kuwait passed on January 15, 1991. The war to evict Iraqi forces began two days later. Iraq lost central control of its air defense network almost immediately, rendering the whole system useless. The loss of central communications systems meant that all surface-to-air missiles, antiaircraft guns, and Iraqi airplanes patrolling the skies over Baghdad were effectively blinded. Adding to this, most Iraqi pilots were not skilled in dogfights (aerial battles between jet planes). Even the elite pilots flying the best French- and Soviet-made jets in the Iraqi inventory were no match for coalition pilots flying the latest American and British fighters. By the end of the first week, the coalition controlled the skies over Iraq.

The first three phases of Desert Storm were so successful they unfolded virtually together. Iraqi infantry and armor around Kuwait were assaulted from the first day by B-52s, attack jets, and artillery and rockets. Eventually, the battleships *Wisconsin* and *Missouri* of the U.S. Navy joined the fight, firing 2,700-pound shells into Iraqi command bunkers and artillery and radar sites. After a month of bombing, Iraqi troops had lost 200,000 men, mostly through desertion (running away from army service) and mass surrenders.

The battleship USS *Wisconsin* fires a round at Iraqi targets in Kuwait during Operation Desert Storm.

An American F-14A Tomcat (front) conducts a patrol mission with a British Royal Air Force Mark 2 Phantom II.

Underestimating the coalition's enormous airpower had been one of the greatest of Saddam's miscalculations. The bombing he thought would last a week ran 39 days, severely damaging his army before the ground war even started. Now, during the ground war, another Iraqi assumption was about to be proven terribly wrong. The western end of Iraq's defense line ended just beyond the point at which the borders of Kuwait, Saudi Arabia, and Iraq met. It should have ended much farther west. Saddam chose to end the defense line where he did, however, for two reasons. First, the Iraqis believed the coalition supply system could not support a mass movement of tanks and troops across 200 miles of harsh desert. Second, in the past the Iraqis had often gotten lost maneuvering in the vastness of that same featureless terrain. They assumed an American-led assault force would flounder, too. Both of these assumptions were incorrect. Coalition troops were well supplied and well organized. They also had the Global Positioning System (GPS), a system of satellites and portable receivers that enabled them to determine their exact location. They would use the GPS with devastating effectiveness.

The "Left Hook"

The coalition ground war began on February 24. Although the coalition's battle plan was simple, its execution would have to be precise. Seventeen thousand U.S. Marines would attack the eastern end of the Iraqi defense line, making it look as if this was the main thrust of the advance. Meanwhile, tens of thousands of soldiers and thousands of tanks would attack the weakest spot in the Iraqis' line—its western end. While the Iraqis on the eastern end of the line were busy fighting a decoy, they would be hit on the west with one of the most powerful armored assaults in history.

The ground attack began at 4:00 A.M. as the Marines slammed into the eastern side of the "Saddam line" and the strongest concentration of Iraqi defenders anywhere in Kuwait. Despite intense fire from defensive artillery and rifles, the Marines breached the line by nightfall and advanced 20 miles. Once their line was broken, the Iraqis surrendered by the thousands.

As the Iraqis were struggling (and failing) to hold the eastern end of their line, the opposite end exploded with the advance of more than 200,000 coalition soldiers and 65,000 vehicles of all types. The U.S. Army's tank-heavy Seventh Corps plowed into the Iraqi line, while the "lighter" Eighteenth Corps (fewer tanks, more infantry) advanced farther west. The Eighteenth was so far beyond the end of the Iraqi line that it charged forward unopposed. Both corps headed north before curving east to get behind the Iraqi forces. On a map, the path of the maneuver suggested a boxer facing north and throwing a great "left hook" at the Iraqi army.

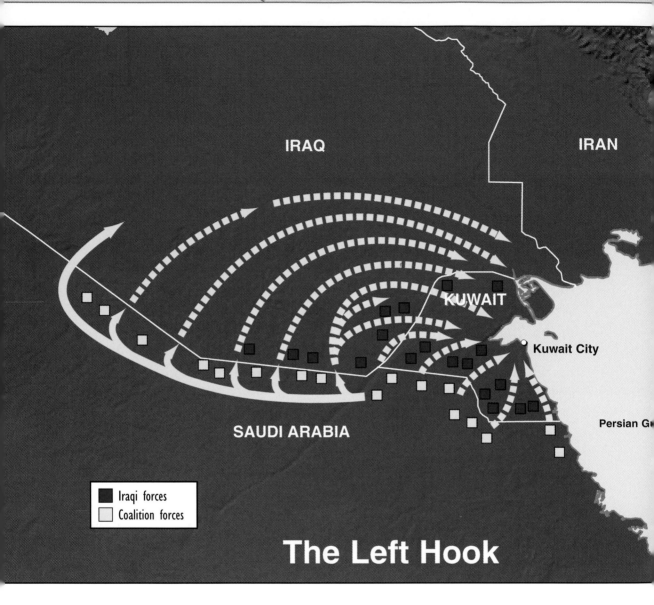

IRAQ

IRAN

KUWAIT

Kuwait City

SAUDI ARABIA

Persian G

■ Iraqi forces
□ Coalition forces

The Left Hook

A map of the "Left Hook" movement made by coalition forces during the ground war

To the east, the Marines achieved their goal on February 26, the third day of the ground phase, as they pushed the last Iraqis out of Kuwait City. At around the same time to the west, the Seventh Corps faced the heaviest fighting of the war. Shocked by the Americans' sudden appearance, the well-trained Republican Guards anchoring that sector fought fiercely (unlike most of the Iraqi army, which fled or surrendered in droves).

The Iraqis' combat skills, as well as their equipment and weaponry, were not as advanced as the coalition force's were, however. Rounds from Iraq's Russian-made T-72 tanks bounced off the front of the American M1A1s even at close range. In contrast, the armor-piercing shells of the M1A1s easily penetrated the T-72s at distances beyond two miles. Hundreds of burning tanks, armored personnel carriers, and trucks littered the battlefield as the Americans raced to block the last routes out of Kuwait. By the end of February 27, Kuwait was surrounded and control of the country had passed into the hands of the coalition. At 8:00 the next morning, President Bush called an end to the fighting.

Top: An Iraqi T-72 main battle tank sits on a battlefield in Kuwait. Bottom: A Marine Corps MIAI Abrams battle tank during the ground phase of Operation Desert Storm. The MIAI weighed 69 tons and was capable of moving at speeds of more than 40 miles per hour.

Kuwaiti oil wells, set on fire by retreating Iraqi forces, fill the sky with a thick, black smoke. More than 700 oil wells were set ablaze during the war.

Aftermath

Militarily, Saddam had suffered a terrible defeat. Over the 43 days of Desert Storm, coalition air forces flew almost 110,000 missions and dropped more than 140,000 tons of bombs. The air war did untold damage to Iraq's war-making capabilities and eliminated an estimated 40 percent of its prewar combat aircraft. This included more than 100 of Iraq's best fighter planes, which Saddam ordered flown to Iran to escape destruction and which the Iranians never returned. Before the ground war had even begun, the air campaign had reduced Iraqi troop strength in Kuwait by one-third and destroyed approximately 1,300 Iraqi tanks. The coalition achieved all this with the loss of only 75 planes.

Iraqi soldiers surrendered in large numbers to coalition troops. The man shown in front here is holding up the Koran, the Muslim holy book.

Twenty-eight Americans were killed when an Iraqi Scud missile destroyed this army barracks in Dhahran, Saudi Arabia, on February 25, 1991.

The Iraqis also used Scuds against the people of Israel and Saudi Arabia. Americans attempted to defend much of Saudi Arabia with Patriot missiles, but in the beginning of the war, Israel was heavily hit. Remarkably, only one Israeli citizen was killed in the attacks. Hundreds, however, were injured, and the damage to homes, businesses, and public property was extensive. In neighborhoods like the one shown in the lower photo, in the Tel Aviv area, an estimated 9,000 homes and apartments were destroyed.

The devastation from the ground war was just as one-sided. When the U.S. Army pushed through on the west, the Iraqis were taken completely unaware. First they had underestimated the coalition's ability to cross miles and miles of barren desert to reach their unprotected flank. Then their surveillance airplanes were grounded by swarming coalition fighters. The Iraqi forces were swept from Kuwait in just 100 hours.

Iraq's human loss during the war was also staggering. About 25,000 Iraqis perished, with as many as 12,000 soldiers and 2,300 civilians dying in the air campaign and another 10,000 soldiers killed during the ground phase. Although exact numbers are difficult to determine, it has been estimated that as many as 86,000 Iraqis were taken prisoner. Coalition losses were much smaller, with 240 soldiers killed in action, including 148 Americans.

Saddam had underestimated the coalition forces, which remained strong and confident throughout the war. The air campaign was not a 7- or 10-day pinprick, but a terrible 39-day sledgehammer that all but smashed the Iraqi army before it could even fight. The ground war, when it came, was not the mother of all battles, but the mother of all retreats by the Iraqis. And there was no negotiation, only apparent humiliation for Saddam Hussein.

Remarkably, Saddam did not think he had lost. He knew that much of the Republican Guard had escaped Kuwait intact. With these loyal troops, Saddam could crush internal opposition and remain in power. General Wafiq al-Samarra'i, Saddam's intelligence chief, later recalled what happened when he phoned Saddam with the news that Bush had called the cease-fire. "He felt himself to be a great, great hero," said Samarra'i. "He started to say, 'We won. We won.' His morale went from zero to 100." And if Saddam's goal had been to take on the greatest military power the world had ever known and survive to fight another day, then he did win.

CHAPTER 3

Containing Iraq
1991-2001

Although the United States-led coalition succeeded in expelling the Iraqi army from Kuwait, it deliberately stopped short of removing Saddam Hussein from power. The United Nations had authorized only Saddam's eviction from Kuwait, not his overthrow. Coalition leaders did not want to invade Iraq to depose Saddam. That would mean occupying the nation, feeding the people, and rebuilding Iraqi society—a very costly and time-consuming endeavor that few countries were prepared to undertake. Instead, the coalition hoped its punishing attack had so weakened Saddam's army and his credibility with his people that he would quickly fall without more fighting.

The Iraqi leader did not fall, however. More of Saddam's army survived the war than the Americans had realized, including most of his loyal Republican Guard. Within weeks of the cease-fire, Saddam crushed uprisings in northern and southern Iraq. About 20,000 Kurds were killed in the north and as many as 2 million fled their homes. Meanwhile, up to 60,000 Iraqi Shi'ah were slaughtered in the south.

As Saddam reasserted his power, the UN took steps to control his aggression with an approach known as containment. The first "brick" in the "wall" to hold back Iraq was laid on April 3, 1991, when the UN Security Council passed Resolution 687. The resolution required Iraq to stop developing weapons of mass destruction—chemical, biological, and nuclear weapons, as well as systems such as ballistic missiles that could

After the Persian Gulf War, millions of Iraqi Kurds fled from Saddam Hussein's army into the mountains of northern Iraq, where many starved or froze to death. In an effort called Operation Provide Comfort, coalition forces gave the refugees food, water, and medicine and built camps to shelter and protect them. U.S. Army helicopters, such as the CH-47 Chinook shown here, helped bring groups of Kurds to the safety of these camps.

A U.S. Air Force F-15E Eagle patrols the no-fly zone over the mountains of northern Iraq. At first, enforcing the northern no-fly zone was part of Operation Provide Comfort, but in 1996 it became known as Operation Northern Watch. (The enforcement of the southern no-fly zone was called Operation Southern Watch.)

deliver them. UN inspectors entered Iraq to find and destroy these weapons. To force Saddam to cooperate with the disarmament, Resolution 687 kept in place the economic sanctions set by the UN after Iraq's invasion of Kuwait.

The U.S. laid another brick in the wall a few days later, when it established a "no-fly" zone in northern Iraq to protect the Kurds. Iraqi aircraft were forbidden to fly in the zone, which was patrolled by American, British, and French jets. A second no-fly zone created over southern Iraq in August 1992 shielded the Shi'ah. The no-fly zones not only helped the Kurds and Shi'ah, but they also provided buffers between Iraq and nations to the north (Turkey and parts of Syria and Iran) and to the south (Saudi Arabia and Kuwait).

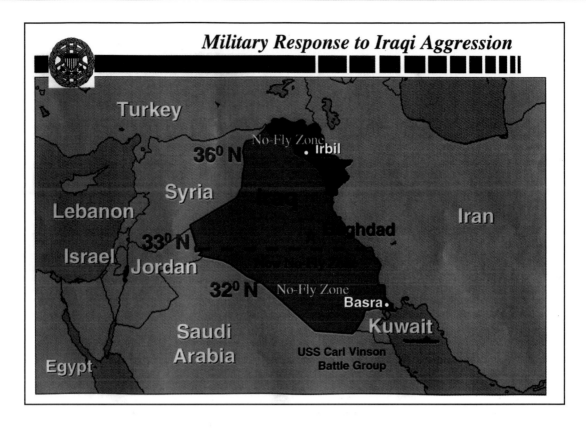

Military Response to Iraqi Aggression

In addition to enforcing the no-fly zones, coalition airpower often punished Saddam when he defied UN dictates. Coalition forces also served to block any future Iraqi invasion of surrounding nations. Together, the inspections, the sanctions, and the U.S.-led military presence formed the strategy of containment—the wall that coalition members hoped would hold back Saddam Hussein.

Trying to Disarm Saddam

Saddam butted against the wall from the beginning. Iraq ignored UN Security Council instructions to repay Kuwait. Saddam also disobeyed UN demands to stop repressing his people, except when military force (such as the enforcement of the no-fly zones) prevented him. To make matters worse, Saddam

A U.S. Department of Defense map of the Iraq no-fly zones as they were in September 1996. The northern zone covered all of Iraq north of 36° north latitude. The southern zone originally lay south of 32° until 1996, when it was extended northward to 33°.

Wearing protective gear, UN weapons inspectors measure the amount of nerve agent in a container found in Iraq in the early 1990s.

resisted disarmament. He ordered Iraqi soldiers to intimidate weapons inspectors. He forced scientists to conceal weapons-related documents or to lie to inspectors outright. He directed officials not to dismantle weapons facilities as the UN ordered. He prompted managers to delay inspections of other facilities for hours, presumably to remove evidence of wrongdoing. While the inspectors did find and destroy tens of thousands of banned weapons, Saddam managed to hide much of (and even build up) his secret stockpile over the next several years.

The first hint that Saddam was outfoxing inspectors came in December 1994, when Wafiq al-Samarra'i, head of Iraq's intelligence service, defected (disowned his country and moved to another). He revealed Iraq's secret development of VX nerve agent and how Saddam had planned to fire the deadly chemical at coalition forces if they had entered Baghdad in 1991. Furthermore, al-Samarra'i said that Iraq had an extensive biological weapons program that continued to operate behind the backs of inspectors. He also admitted that Saddam was hiding chemical and biological warheads, along with more than 40 Scud ballistic missiles capable of delivering them.

Inspectors were in for another rude awakening in August 1995. Hussein Kamel, Saddam Hussein's son-in-law and head of development of weapons of mass destruction, defected to Jordan, leading to the discovery of some 650,000 documents related to Iraq's weapons program. The evidence showed that Iraq had deceived the UN all along by continuing to develop

Hussein Kamel in August 1995. He returned to Iraq with his brother, Saddam Kamel, on February 20, 1996. Three days later, both men were assassinated.

nuclear warheads to fit atop Scuds. Hussein Kamel also told officials about a biological weapons factory at a facility that only recently had passed inspection. Thirty thousand liters of anthrax and botulinum toxins were among the biological agents the "clean" plant had produced.

A third high-level defector confirmed that Saddam could and did fool the inspectors. In 1995, Khidir Hamza, a nuclear scientist who helped found Iraq's nuclear weapons program in the early 1970s, defected to the U.S. His description of the lies that cloaked Saddam's atomic ambition was chilling. "The problem with trying to learn the truth about the Iraqi nuclear weapons program," wrote Hamza, "is the complete secrecy and the security measures that surround it. The movements of insiders, including members of their families, are restricted, and breaking the rules can be a death sentence. Muayad Naji, a centrifuge program worker, left Iraq without authorization in 1992. He was shot down by Iraqi intelligence agents on a street in Amman, Jordan, in front of his wife and children." Hamza warned: "What is not recognized by the world community . . . is the determination with which the regime of Saddam Hussein intends to pursue programs to produce weapons of mass destruction, including nuclear weapons, once sanctions are lifted. The nuclear weapons group is still in place; the expertise is still there; and Saddam Hussein and his colleagues are well practiced in the arts of deception."

Hamza's comments revealed a major shortcoming of the weapons inspections. Regardless of what was found, no number of inspections could ever change Saddam's *intention* to build banned weapons. As Hamza pointed out, Saddam fully planned to build nuclear arms as soon as trade restrictions were lifted and he could acquire the necessary material.

A second complaint many experts had about inspections was that evidence was very difficult—if not impossible—to find, and interpretations of what was found often conflicted. By the late 1990s, it was clear to many observers that Saddam was hiding weapons. But the International Atomic Energy Agency (IAEA), which looked for nuclear weapons in Iraq on behalf of the UN, found no proof. On October 13, 1998, IAEA director-general Mohammed ElBaradei reported that he saw "no indication that Iraq has assembled nuclear weapons" and that he believed "Iraq's known nuclear weapons related assets have been destroyed, removed or rendered harmless." Responding to ElBaradei's report, two experts pointed to what they believed was good evidence from a chief weapons inspector that Saddam did have the necessary parts to build three nuclear devices. The IAEA, they said, had either missed the clues or mistakenly dismissed them. "The threat of an Iraqi nuclear breakout remains real," wrote the two experts, Paul Leventhal and Steven Dolley, in the *Washington Post* on November 29, 1998. "The prudent assumption for the IAEA should be that Iraq's nuclear program continues, and that the Iraqis may now lack only the fissile material"—the enriched uranium or plutonium to produce a nuclear explosion.

Leventhal and Dolley's warning was especially alarming because at that moment the whole inspection process was crumbling. Saddam had resisted inspections on many occasions. Three times he evicted inspectors outright: in November 1997, January 1998, and November 1998. The first two times, the situation was resolved and inspectors returned. The last incident ended differently. It led to a series of air and cruise missile strikes by American and British forces to punish Saddam and to destroy suspected weapons facilities. Known as Operation Desert Fox, the attack lasted several days, from December 16 to December 19, 1998. Soon afterward, Iraq broke off all contact with UN weapons inspectors. Although evidence was mounting that Saddam's nuclear weapons program was within sight of success, the inspectors did not return for four years.

Limiting Trade

As inspections fell apart in late 1998, another brick cracked in the wall of containment. The UN had first applied trade sanctions in August 1990 to force Saddam to leave Kuwait. The sanctions forbade all trade with Iraq except for supplies needed by the Iraqi people, such as food and medicine. The idea was to impoverish Saddam, to cut him off from weapons, industrial machinery, spare truck parts—anything that he could use to maintain power. Sanctions had not worked by the time of Operation Desert Storm in January 1991. After the cease-fire ending the war, the UN kept the embargo in place to prod Saddam to disarm. It made clear that if he disarmed, the restrictions would be lifted.

The idea of sanctions for Iraq had always been controversial. The main complaint was that sanctions hurt the Iraqi people more than Saddam, the true target. Although the sanctions never prohibited imports of medicine or food, Iraq insisted the restrictions starved the Iraqi people and caused a health crisis. According to Iraq's ambassador to the UN, sanctions were the real "weapon of mass destruction. From 1990, when sanctions were imposed on Iraq, until 1995, half a million children under the age of five died of malnutrition and preventable diseases." This "artificial famine," Iraq claimed, had left "a third of Iraq's surviving children [with] stunted growth and nutritional deficiencies that will deform their shortened lives."

Studies conducted by the UN and the U.S., however, indicated that more than enough food and medicine was available for Iraq to purchase. If Saddam was short of funds to buy these goods, it was not the UN's fault. On August 15, 1991, the Security Council had authorized Iraq to sell oil and use the proceeds for food and other humanitarian items. But it was not until nearly five years later, on May 20, 1996, that Saddam accepted the deal. Although it is impossible to know why he waited so long, the likeliest reason is that he hoped to gain sympathy from the international community, which might then

Top: An F/A-18C Hornet prepares to take off from the deck of the USS *Enterprise* on an air strike against Iraq as part of Operation Desert Fox. Bottom: An officer aboard the *Enterprise* monitors another plane's takeoff.

Iraqi workers sit by sacks of imported goods purchased under the UN oil-for-food program.

ease the sanctions or cancel them outright. He finally accepted aid only when conditions grew so bad that Iraqi citizens threatened revolution.

The oil-for-food program did help the Iraqi people. Still, as Iraq earned more and more money from oil over the next several years, living conditions among common Iraqis remained surprisingly low. Saddam was not spending enough of the money on the people. Evidence showed that food and medicine were routinely smuggled out of Iraq and sold at a profit on the black market. Even as the media printed photos and statistics of starving Iraqi children, baby food from Iraq turned up in neighboring countries. In a typical incident, a shipment of 2,000 metric tons of rice was caught being shipped out of the country, for sale by the Iraqi government. While this was happening, Saddam managed to pay for the construction of more than 40 presidential palaces.

Still, Saddam's anti-sanctions propaganda campaign had the desired effect. On December 17, 1999, the UN Security Council erased the limit on the amount of oil Iraq could sell and ended the ban on most of the items Iraq had been forbidden to import (although the ban on weapons remained in effect). The annual oil-for-food revenue stood at about $17 billion by the end of 1999. Since Iraq now had more money to buy a greater variety of goods, easing the sanctions benefited its trade partners, too. France and Russia, for example, signed more oil-for-food contracts than any other nations. Not surprisingly, both countries supported either easing the sanctions further or lifting them altogether. China, likewise, profited from oil-for-food contracts. The fact that these nations—a majority of the five permanent members of the UN's ruling Security Council—had a great economic interest in seeing the sanctions lifted did not bode well for the future of the restrictions. (The United States and Britain are the other two permanent members.)

Unfortunately, not all income from oil sales went to buy food or other goods allowed by UN guidelines. Money Iraq earned as part of the oil-for-food program was supposed to go directly into a UN-managed account that Iraq then drew upon to buy approved goods. In 2000, however, Saddam was able to get his hands on about five percent of the income by smuggling some of Iraq's oil to neighbors such as Syria, Jordan, and Turkey, outside UN channels. The following year, illegal trade accounted for 15 to 20 percent of Iraq's total oil income. By 2002, Saddam was earning about $3 billion annually to spend on anything nations were willing to send across Iraq's borders—including banned weapons.

Striking with Military Force

The containment strategy was falling apart. Inspections had been ended and sanctions were quickly following. The other brick in the wall, the American-led military presence, was still operating but with ever-greater restrictions. In the first years after the Gulf War, it had been able to quickly counter Iraqi defiance. When Saddam harassed weapons inspectors in early January 1993, the UN authorized air and cruise missile strikes by coalition forces. The attacks leveled Iraqi air defense sites, from which Saddam's military had threatened coalition jets patrolling the southern no-fly zone, and a factory outside Baghdad suspected of being part of Iraq's nuclear weapons program. In April 1993, Saddam plotted to assassinate George H. W. Bush while the former president visited Kuwait. Although the scheme failed, the U.S. responded on June 27 by destroying the headquarters of the Iraqi intelligence service (which had planned the assassination) with cruise missiles launched from warships in the Persian Gulf.

International support for military action against Iraq waned over the next few years. In 1996, Saddam launched a brutal crackdown on the northern Kurds, again violating the UN's order not to repress the Iraqi people. The coalition planned to respond with airstrikes, but Saudi Arabia, Turkey, and Jordan—three nations that bordered Iraq—refused to allow coalition jets to launch from bases in their countries. The U.S. and Great Britain had to settle for less effective cruise missile hits. This demonstrated the growing discomfort many Arab nations felt in supporting America's tough stand on Iraq. Even though none of the Arab nations around Iraq were true democracies, the voices of the people were heard loud and clear by their leaders. Iraqis were suffering unduly from sanctions and military strikes that seemed to have no end, and their Arab neighbors were not going to allow the situation to continue much longer.

Many Arab leaders had reason to hate Saddam Hussein. But by the end of the 1990s, they were privately telling the U.S. that

they could only hold support together for one final, decisive invasion to remove Saddam. What none of them could continue to do was support indefinite sanctions, punitive airstrikes, and a large American military presence—in other words, containment. Public opinion simply would no longer allow it. The wall around Saddam was crumbling.

From the Persian Gulf, the USS *Shiloh* launches a cruise missile against Iraq in September 1996 as part of Operation Desert Strike, the response to Saddam's attack on the Kurds.

CHAPTER 4

The Buildup to War 2001-2003

On September 11, 2001, members of Osama bin Laden's al-Qaeda terrorist network flew two airliners filled with highly explosive jet fuel into the World Trade Center complex in New York City and one into the Pentagon (the headquarters of the Defense Department) outside Washington, D.C. The twin towers of the World Trade Center collapsed and a portion of the Pentagon was destroyed. About 3,000 people were killed, including airline passengers and crew members, office workers, and the 19 hijackers. A fourth passenger jet, American Airlines Flight 93, crashed in a Pennsylvania field on its way to Washington, after heroic passengers fought the hijackers for control of the plane. Their sacrifice saved hundreds more who would have died had the flying bomb reached its target—perhaps the White House or the Capitol.

The horrifying events of September 11 caused a major shift in the way the United States responded to threats to its national security. Before the attacks, it had relied on a strategy of deterrence. It warned potential foes that their aggression would trigger a military response, and it retaliated if the aggression continued. (In extreme cases, the response could be nuclear, although that happened only once—against Japan to end World War II.) Deterrence worked for decades against the former Soviet Union, America's adversary during the Cold War. It also helped to contain Iraq from 1991 to 2003. The leaders of both nations carefully weighed the possible gains from aggression

The destroyed World Trade Center (top) and the damaged Pentagon after the terrorist attacks of September 11, 2001

against the likely U.S. response. When the gain did not seem worth the cost, they backed off. Deterrence failed on September 11, however. The hijackers did not fear retaliation. They wanted to die for their cause. The only way the attacks could have been prevented was to keep the terrorists from gaining access to the airplanes in the first place.

Had the hijackings been an isolated event—a one-time shot by a small group working alone—the U.S. might not have overhauled its defense strategy. But al-Qaeda was a vast network of operatives with a history of anti-American violence, including the 1993 bombing of the World Trade Center and the 2000 bombing of the USS *Cole* off the coast of Yemen. The organization crisscrossed the globe and included many potential suicide bombers. Just 19 members had killed thousands of people in minutes using nothing more than four airplanes. The next group of terrorists might get their hands on far deadlier weapons—nerve agents, bacteria, or nuclear devices—and kill tens or hundreds of thousands. To meet this threat, President George W. Bush unveiled a strategy that no longer relied on deterrence alone. Instead, it sought to repeat, on a global scale, what the passengers of Flight 93 did over Pennsylvania on September 11—stop the terrorists from gaining control of the weapons.

The Bush Doctrine

In several speeches after the September 11 attacks, Bush announced his new approach, which became known as the "Bush Doctrine." The greatest threat to the United States, he said, was the union of weapons of mass destruction with three radical elements: global terrorist networks such as al-Qaeda, weak nations that harbored terrorists (like Afghanistan, which sheltered al-Qaeda), and rogue nations. Rogue nations are those that operate outside international law. Bush considered them especially dangerous. "States like these, and their terrorist allies," he said in his January 2002 State of the Union

address, "constitute an axis of evil, arming to threaten the peace of the world. By seeking weapons of mass destruction, these regimes pose a grave and growing danger. They could provide these arms to terrorists, giving them the means to match their hatred. They could attack our allies or attempt to blackmail the United States. In any of these cases, the price of indifference would be catastrophic."

Even as Bush spoke, America and its allies were making war on al-Qaeda and Afghanistan, the first two elements targeted by the Bush Doctrine. In July 2002, the U.S. began a military

George W. Bush giving his State of the Union address on January 29, 2002. "Our nation is at war, our economy is in recession, and the civilized world faces unprecedented dangers," he said.

A propaganda poster of al-Qaeda leader Osama bin Laden, found by U.S. Navy SEALs in Afghanistan

buildup against what Bush considered one of the major rogue nations—Saddam Hussein's Iraq. Saddam had been developing weapons of mass destruction since the mid-1970s. He had used chemical weapons against foes both foreign (the Iranians) and domestic (the Kurds). More than a decade after the United Nations first ordered him to disarm, Saddam continued to stockpile chemicals, bacteria, ballistic missiles, and the equipment and material needed to build nuclear bombs. He had invaded his neighbors (Iran and Kuwait). He tortured and starved his own people. He also sponsored international terror-ism and was believed to have links to al-Qaeda. Although Iraq was not implicated in the September 11 attacks, the Bush Doctrine demanded that Iraq be confronted.

At first, the world seemed to agree. On November 8, 2002, all 15 members of the UN Security Council approved Resolution 1441, which required Saddam to give up his banned weapons programs. It was the latest in a long line of similar res-olutions stretching back to 1991. Iraq was ordered to cooperate "immediately, unconditionally, and actively" in a new round of inspections. In October, the U.S. Congress had authorized

The UN Security council voting to approve Resolution 1441

Bush to enforce the UN resolutions regarding Iraq, with armed force if necessary. Bush believed he now had legal justification to overthrow Saddam if the Iraqi dictator refused this last chance to disarm.

As the weapons inspections continued over the next several months, however, international and domestic opposition to a second war against Saddam grew. One of the earliest and strongest objections to war focused on the legality of the Bush Doctrine itself. In international law, a nation has the right to launch a first (or "preemptive") strike against another nation only if it can prove it is about to be attacked by that nation. This type of danger is known as "imminent threat." In 1837, U.S. secretary of state Daniel Webster established the legal standard for imminent threat that the world community still recognizes: the danger had to be "instant, overwhelming, leaving no choice of means and no moment for deliberation." For a preemptive strike to be considered legal, the hostile nation must show the intention of launching an attack.

Bush challenged Webster's standard. As he explained in June 2002, "If we wait for threats to fully materialize, we will have waited too long." In Bush's opinion, Americans could no longer live with the old definition of imminent threat. There had been no advance warning of the September 11 attacks. If the terrorists had used chemical, biological, or nuclear weapons, the destruction they caused could have been infinitely worse. Bush believed the U.S. could not wait for future threats to become obvious. He therefore adopted a new definition of imminent threat. It no longer meant a nation's intention to attack, but rather its capability. As long as a country could attack the U.S. and had shown by past actions or words that it might attack in the future, Bush could consider it an imminent threat and order a preemptive strike.

Critics believed Bush's new strategy was illegal. What someone might do years in the future was simply impossible to know, they argued. What the Bush Doctrine advocated—making war on a nation today because it might attack tomorrow—was the definition of "preventive" war, which is not considered legal. *Washington Post* columnist William Raspberry made this point in September 2002. "What threat has Iraq uttered against us to justify the war talk that permeates Washington these days?" he asked. He and others questioned Iraq's capability or intention of attacking the U.S. with any type of weapon.

Debate in the UN

Despite opposition, the U.S. military buildup continued. By the end of 2002, 60,000 soldiers, 400 aircraft, and 2 aircraft carriers had been deployed to the Middle East. Britain, America's strongest international supporter, planned to send 17 ships to

Prime Minister Tony Blair (left) reinforced Britain's strong support for George W. Bush and the United States in appearances such as this one, a press conference in Crawford, Texas, in April 2002.

the region—its largest naval task force in 20 years. British ground forces would also deploy to the area. But as the strength of the invasion force increased, so did dissent from abroad. France, Russia, and China, the other three permanent members of the UN Security Council, voiced their opposition. They still wanted Saddam to be disarmed, but peacefully, through the inspections process headed by Hans Blix and Mohamed ElBaradei. As chief of the UN Monitoring, Verification, and Inspection Committee (UNMOVIC), Blix searched for Iraq's chemical and biological weapons and ballistic missiles. ElBaradei, head of the International Atomic Energy Agency (IAEA), looked for nuclear weapons. Over the next three months, both inspectors noted Saddam's increasing coopera-tion. For example, when Blix found that Iraq's "Al Samoud 2" ballistic missile exceeded the UN range limit of 93 miles, Saddam agreed to destroy all 120 missiles. Meanwhile, ElBaradei insisted he was finding no proof that Iraq was devel-oping nuclear weapons.

Secretary of State Colin Powell (top) presented the UN Security Council with what he called "solid" evidence that Iraq had not disarmed. His audience included (below) UN Secretary-General Kofi Annan (left), chief weapons inspector Hans Blix (center), and IAEA director Mohamed ElBaradei. Despite Powell's efforts, the U.S. failed to win the support of the Security Council for an invasion of Iraq.

American and British officials, however, doubted the sinceri-ty of Saddam's cooperation. They considered it a ploy to buy time and split the UN Security Council. They, too, found sup-port for their views in Blix's reports. In January 2003, for instance, Blix told the UN that "Iraq appears not to have come to a genuine acceptance—not even today—of the disarmament, which was demanded of it." Two months later, Blix reported Saddam's failure to account for enormous amounts of chemical and biological agents that inspectors believed existed but could not find. According to U.S. Secretary of State Colin Powell, speaking to the UN Security Council on February 5, the miss-ing agents included more than 6,000 gallons of anthrax-causing bacteria and 1,000 tons of chemicals such as mustard gas. Blix added 5,000 gallons of botulinum toxin to the list in March. In Bush's judgment, Saddam had thrown away his last chance to disarm.

Moving Closer to War

An invasion force of a quarter-million U.S. and British soldiers ringed Iraq by March. In the past, Saddam had bent only to superior force—and sometimes not even then. Bush and his advisers believed Saddam would not be taking any steps toward disarmament now if not for the troops gathering on Iraq's borders. Bush feared that Saddam would stop disarming, and even rearm, if the force left without invading. The costs of deploying to the Persian Gulf had been extraordinary, both in money and in relations with other countries. The U.S. could not afford another buildup. As Bush saw the situation in March 2003, it was then or never to remove Saddam from power.

Meanwhile, opposition to war continued to build. Some Americans felt that the Bush administration's focus on Saddam was jeopardizing success in the war against terrorism. To former secretary of state Madeleine Albright, it was a question of America's limited resources being stretched too thinly: "It makes little sense now to focus the world's attention and our own military, intelligence, diplomatic, and financial resources on a plan to invade Iraq instead of on al-Qaeda's ongoing plans to murder innocent people. We cannot fight a second monumental struggle without detracting from the first one." Brent Scowcroft—who had been national security advisor to Bush's father, President George H. W. Bush—also recognized America's inability to fight terrorism alone. Tracking down terrorists required the intelligence, financial, and human resources of many nations. Scowcroft worried that an invasion would be so unpopular that other countries would stop giving the U.S. the help it needed.

The Bush administration, however, maintained that the war against Saddam was the war against terror. "You can't distinguish between al-Qaeda and Saddam when you talk about the war on terrorism," the president declared in September 2002. "They're both equally as bad, and equally as evil, and equally as destructive." The enormous costs of fighting them simply had

to be borne—alone, if necessary. Bush rejected the notion that France, Russia, or any other country should decide how the U.S. responded to threats to its national security. "When it comes to our security, we really don't need anybody's permission," he said. "My job is to protect America, and that's exactly what I'm going to do." Invading Iraq could prevent Saddam's banned weapons from ending up in the hands of terrorists and being used to attack the U.S. Bush also hoped that deposing Saddam would promote peace in the Middle East, especially if a democracy rose in his place.

In Los Angeles on October 6, 2002, at least 5,000 people marched to protest the Bush administration's policy toward Iraq. Millions more protested in cities in the U.S. and around the world as the buildup to war continued.

In addition to fearing further terrorist attacks, Bush worried that Saddam would use nuclear weapons to dominate the Persian Gulf oil supply. This would devastate not only the U.S. economy, but also the economy of the entire world. Bush supported the well-established policy outlined in the Eisenhower and Carter Doctrines—that no nation should be allowed to disrupt the free flow of Persian Gulf oil. Bush's father fought Iraq in 1991 primarily to uphold the same policy. As George W. Bush's critics pointed out in 2003, however, U.S. and British companies stood to profit the most from another war with Iraq. In January of that year, 10 percent of U.S. oil imports came from Iraq. The U.S. and British oil companies that imported the oil bought it from other countries first, then passed it on to U.S. consumers. This was profitable, but not as much as controlling at least some of the oil at its source. Iraq had proven reserves of 112 billion barrels, second in the world after Saudi Arabia's 262 billion. With Saddam in power, though, American and British companies had no access to these reserves. He would not award rich oil-drilling contracts to countries that worked against him in the UN. A regime change in Iraq would finally give U.S. and British companies direct access to Iraqi oil, leading to handsome profits.

Supporters of a war against Iraq downplayed the obvious American and British economic motivation to invade. Instead, they pointed to the financial reasons France, Russia, and China had to block Saddam's overthrow. In some cases, these nations held contracts to develop Iraqi oil worth hundreds of billions of dollars. They could lose these contracts if Saddam were removed from power. Furthermore, all three countries had been Saddam's major suppliers of military hardware before the UN sanctions blocked weapons transfers to Iraq in 1991. And all three were among Iraq's top trading partners in the years after the Gulf War. No nations would have profited more from the full resumption of trade with a Saddam-controlled Iraq.

By mid-March 2003, President Bush and his advisors had given up on the UN inspections process. It was clear to them that Saddam Hussein would never give up his weapons of mass destruction willingly. And if the U.S. were forced to withdraw its military units from the region without invading, there would be no one left to force the Iraqi tyrant to disarm. Bush made his decision. On the evening of March 17, he issued Saddam an ultimatum: leave Iraq in 48 hours or face destruction at the hands of the 300,000 American and British soldiers waiting on Iraq's borders. "The United States of America has the sovereign authority to use force in assuring its own national security," Bush said. "That duty falls to me as commander in chief by the oath I have sworn, by the oath I will keep." Two days later, the war began.

USS *Harry S. Truman,* stationed in the Mediterranean Sea, was one of five U.S. Navy aircraft carriers poised for war in March 2003. Each ship was capable of launching 50 of the world's deadliest fighters and ground attack jets.

CHAPTER 5

Operation Iraqi Freedom 2003

A coalition led by the United States and Great Britain invaded Iraq on March 20, 2003. In a press conference the following day, U.S. Defense Secretary Donald Rumsfeld listed eight specific objectives guiding the coalition military campaign, called Operation Iraqi Freedom: 1) to overthrow the regime of Saddam Hussein; 2) to eliminate Iraq's weapons of mass destruction; 3) to capture terrorists living in Iraq; 4) to collect intelligence about regional and global terrorist networks; 5) to collect intelligence related to the global network of weapons of mass destruction; 6) to deliver food, medicine, and other humanitarian aid to the Iraqi people; 7) to secure Iraq's oil fields for the people; and 8) to help the Iraqis build a democratic government.

No word captures the essence of the war to oust Saddam better than "speed." Everything about the campaign unfolded like a videotape played on "fast forward." It even began earlier than expected. The original plan called for the invasion to start Friday, March 21. On March 19, however, U.S. intelligence sources (two Iraqi officers recruited from Saddam's inner circle) unexpectedly pinpointed the whereabouts of the dictator and other senior officials in Baghdad. President Bush ordered a "decapitation" strike of precision-guided bombs and cruise missiles against the leaders of the Iraqi regime. Saddam escaped, but he was badly shaken in the bombing. In a disordered appearance on Iraqi television soon afterwards, he

Secretary of Defense Donald Rumsfeld briefs the media following the first strike in Operation Iraqi Freedom.

rambled, seemed confused, and often lost his place while reading his speech. A U.S. official noted that the attack must have left Saddam "wondering about the loyalty of some of those around him."

Saddam's associates must have realized how bad he looked. Fearing an uprising by the Iraqi people should the regime appear weak, and hoping to intimidate the coalition, they sent Information Minister Muhammad Said al-Sahhaf before the foreign press. Self-confident and defiant, he called the Americans "stupid" and "criminals." He vowed that Iraq's response to the bombing "has not started yet, you'll see. In 1991, we saw a much larger scale of military action than we have seen now. We can absorb all military threats." Many Westerners unfamiliar with al-Sahhaf were unsure what to think. Was he all bluff, or

Muhammad Said al-Sahhaf gives a press conference following the coalition's first attack against Saddam's regime.

did he know something the rest of them did not, like whether Saddam's regime would counter the strike with chemical or biological attacks?

General Tommy Franks, the commander-in-chief of U.S. Central Command, felt the anxiety, too. In planning the campaign, he believed he had to strike fast to avoid any of several "nightmare" scenarios that might play out during the invasion. His biggest worry was that Saddam would launch chemical weapons at coalition troops, or at Israel, which might retaliate and draw other Arab nations into the conflict. Repeating what he had done in Kuwait in 1991, Saddam could torch Iraq's 1,000 or so oil wells, causing an environmental disaster and greatly increasing the cost of postwar reconstruction. Saddam might order dams blown up, flooding coalition forces and forcing them to deal with thousands of displaced civilians. Still another fear was that Iraqi troops would destroy the bridges over the Tigris and Euphrates Rivers, which the coalition would have to cross to reach Baghdad.

Franks intended for coalition troops to overrun the country and capture Baghdad before the Iraqi leadership could execute its destructive plans. He promised a "campaign unlike any other in history . . . characterized by shock, by surprise, by flexibility and by the employment of precise munitions on a scale never before seen, and by the application of overwhelming force." The Iraqis would struggle to meet opposition coming from every direction—"shock and awe from day one," as one U.S. officer put it.

But Franks's plan carried enormous risks. One was to the coalition's supply line. To converge on Baghdad with enough speed and strength, ground forces could not occupy every urban area along the way. As a result, Iraqi guerrilla forces, called "irregulars," could hole up in bypassed towns and harass the coalition's supply line to Kuwait. Everything the troops needed to make war—fuel, ammunition, food, water—would be vulnerable. A second risk involved "friendly fire." With British and

U.S. air forces flying hundreds of missions a day above Iraq, tens of thousands of coalition soldiers rushing forward on the ground, and hundreds of commandos operating behind enemy lines, some of the "friendlies" were bound to be targeted by mistake. Yet another risk was the plan's heavy reliance on the commandos. These special forces were mostly U.S. and British, but also Polish and Australian. Just about everywhere regular coalition units would go, commandos had to get there first—to secure missile sites, bridges, and dams, and to identify targets for the air and ground attacks.

In reality, none of these risks could be avoided. Their effects could only be reduced. The best Franks could do was push his subordinate commanders—Lieutenant General Michael "Buzz" Moseley of the U.S. Air Force, the air war commander, and Lieutenant General David McKiernan of the U.S. Army, the ground commander—to coordinate the coalition's every movement as precisely as possible. Franks hoped their best would be good enough.

Marching towards Baghdad

The coalition ground offensive that began on March 20 unfolded in three phases, called "pulses" for the surge of movement that characterized each. The first pulse was a 250-mile dash from the border of Kuwait, where coalition ground forces were based, northward to within about 50 miles of Baghdad. The armies rolled forward in two great columns. The U.S. Army's 3rd Infantry Division formed the bulk of forces on the left. The U.S. Marine Corps's 1st Marine Expeditionary Force, including the 1st Marine Division, joined British units on the right. The left wing headed northwest in a headlong sprint up the Euphrates River, its goal to reach Baghdad as soon as possible. The right moved north toward Basra and the Tigris River.

The right's main objective in the first pulse was to capture a triangle of land known as the Al Faw Peninsula. The Al Faw region's borders were formed by the cities of Basra and Umm

Qasr, and by the southernmost tip of Iraq where it met the Persian Gulf. Just 75 miles long, this finger of land was home to agriculture, livestock, and much of Iraq's oil industry. The right column's immediate mission was to secure these rich oil fields. Part of the force pushed toward Basra, while a portion descended on Umm Qasr, a town that was the end point of Iraq's main oil pipeline and one of the country's main outlets to the Persian Gulf. Still another group of soldiers, made up of

The arrows on this map show the major movements of coalition troops during Operation Iraqi Freedom.

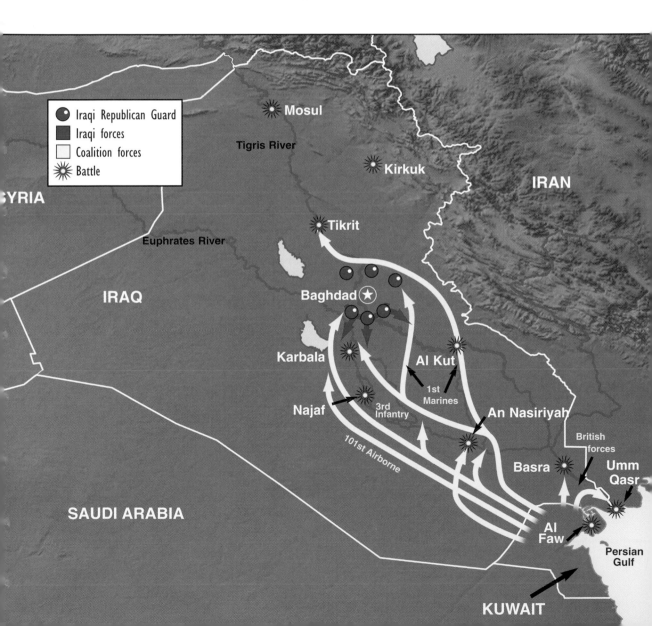

British Royal Marine commandos, raided the remainder of the peninsula. By the second day of the war, the peninsula and its oil fields were secure. So was the port of Umm Qasr, although isolated fighting continued in portions of the town itself. Basra, too, remained contested in places. Iraqi resistance prevented the flow of relief aid, especially drinking water, and within days both cities threatened to become humanitarian disasters.

The problem was not the Iraqi army. Saddam had divided his army into three parts—the regular army, the Republican Guard, and the Special Republican Guard. The regular army, which the coalition expected to face in the initial pulse, was known to be a poor fighting force. Although they numbered about 400,000 men, two-thirds of the regulars were draftees and most had outdated equipment and weapons. Morale was terrible. On the second day of the invasion, the entire 51st Army Division, an estimated 8,000 Iraqi soldiers, either deserted or surrendered. Actually, coalition leaders expected this. U.S. "psy-ops" (psychological operations) units had dropped thousands of leaflets on the Iraqis urging them to give up: "Leave now and go home," read one. "Watch your children learn, grow, and prosper." The alternative was obliteration.

The fighters who resisted the coalition in Basra, Umm Qasr, and several points along the way to Baghdad were not regulars, but irregular guerrilla fighters like the Fedayeen Saddam ("Saddam's men of sacrifice" or "Saddam's martyrs"). Estimates of their numbers ranged from 10,000 to 40,000. Although they were too lightly armed (mostly just automatic weapons and shoulder-fired, rocket-propelled grenades, called "RPGs") to block the coalition's drive to Baghdad, they could slow it somewhat. They fought coalition troops outright in many cases, while at other times they settled for sneak attacks on the coalition's supply line. Still another of the Fedayeen's delaying tactics was to terrorize the towns the coalition bypassed, sometimes through executions. This prevented the mass uprisings the coalition was hoping for to speed the collapse of Saddam's regime.

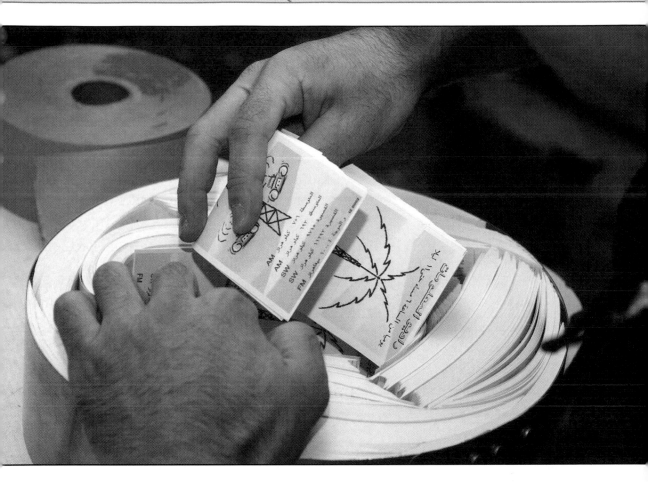

While British troops and U.S. Marines fought irregulars around Umm Qasr and Basra, the 1st Marine Division battled Fedayeen fighters at An Nasiriyah, which straddled the Euphrates River about 225 miles south of Baghdad. (The 1st Marines had left Basra to join the advance to the Iraqi capital.) Franks needed the two bridges at An Nasiriyah. His plan was to send the marines across the Euphrates, where part of the force would continue on to Baghdad along that river. The other part would push north to Al Kut and the Tigris River. From there, the marines would turn left (west) toward Baghdad. With the army's 3rd Infantry Division and part of the 1st Marines moving up the Euphrates, and the rest of the marines

"Psy-ops" leaflets are loaded into canisters to be dropped over Iraq. These particular leaflets urged Iraqis to listen to radio broadcasts about the war, as well as warning them not to attempt to shoot at coalition aircraft.

rolling up the Tigris, Franks would squeeze the city from two directions—a classic "pincer" maneuver. The Americans captured the bridges on March 23, after a day of firefights and mortar duels that cost several marines their lives.

What the marines found in An Nasiriyah after the battle put them on edge—3,000 Iraqi chemical protective suits and stocks of atropine, a nerve agent antidote. In a separate find at a nearby airbase, they discovered more chemical suits and equipment used for chemical decontamination. At still another site in the south, British troops found chemical protective suits in an Iraqi command post. Since the Americans had no chemical weapons, these stockpiles implied the Iraqis themselves had planned to use the banned arms.

A marine kicks open a door as coalition forces search a building in An Nasiriyah.

The Threatening Storm

Meanwhile, the war continued on other fronts. From the air, coalition jets steadily bombarded targets in and around Baghdad, including Republican Guard units. On March 21 alone, American and British ships and submarines fired hundreds of cruise missiles. Air attacks struck the northern city of Mosul, which, along with Kirkuk to its southeast, was a major oil-producing site. On the ground, more than 9,000 commandos and civilian paramilitary operatives from America's Central Intelligence Agency (CIA) moved against targets in every corner of Iraq. Covert teams captured missile sites and airfields in the west, coordinated Kurdish attacks on Iraqi army units in the north, secured oil-producing facilities in the south, and identified targets for coalition air and ground attacks throughout the country. Some of the commandos were assassins sent into urban areas, including Baghdad itself, to eliminate senior leaders. The objective of these squads was as much psychological as physical—to rattle the elite into making mistakes in the war or even turning on Saddam.

The war had its lighter moments. After U.S. and British troops captured the port of Umm Qasr on March 21, Western audiences gained a truer understanding of Information Minister Muhammad Said al-Sahhaf. Apparently, al-Sahhaf was incapable of telling the truth. Even as the American flag flew over Umm Qasr, al-Sahhaf insisted the town was "completely in our hands" and that the coalition "failed to capture it." The sight of British ships docking at Umm Qasr with humanitarian aid did nothing to convince him otherwise. What was really happening, he said, was that "imperialist sheep" were sending out lies and misinformation. As for televised images of surrendering Iraqis: "These are not Iraqi soldiers. They are not members of any of the Iraqi armed forces." His comments were weird, even comical, and they only grew more bizarre as the coalition approached Baghdad.

Members of the army's 3rd Infantry Division assume firing positions as they prepare for battle on their way towards Baghdad.

By March 22, the army's 3rd Infantry Division had reached Samawa on the Euphrates, the halfway point to Baghdad. Three days later, the division was about 50 miles from the capital. Some 7,000 vehicles took part in the movement, including more than 600 M1 Abrams tanks and 400 M2 and M3 Bradley armored personnel carriers. U.S. officials called it the largest, fastest-moving armored column in history. While some Iraqi regulars offered fierce resistance, most simply abandoned their posts. About 7,000 surrendered, including Ahmed Ghobashi, a colonel from Baghdad. "I've got a rifle from World War II," he told his captors. "What can I do against American airplanes?"

There were, in fact, only two things that could stop the coalition. One was the weather. As the 3rd Infantry Division drew near Karbala on March 25, and the 1st Marines concentrated near Al Kut, about 100 miles from Baghdad on the Tigris, a powerful sandstorm blew up. Visibility dropped to 50 yards and most of the coalition's planes and helicopters remained grounded. Marine Gunnery Sergeant Bob Gray recalled it as the worst storm he had seen in two years in the Middle East. If the storm persisted, the advance could falter.

Coalition aircraft aboard the USS *Kitty Hawk* sit grounded during a strong sandstorm.

The other thing that threatened to stop the army was self-doubt. Fedayeen kept attacking the coalition's lengthening supply tail, forcing combat units to peel away from the main force to protect shipments of food, water, ammunition, and fuel. Irregulars continued to strike in towns along the invasion route, like Basra, where a local uprising against the Baathist regime was quickly quashed by the Fedayeen. Reporters and military analysts questioned whether Franks's combat force, at fewer than 100,000 soldiers, was large enough to accomplish the mission. Better to stop, they advised him, secure your supply lines, and await reinforcements. The Fedayeen might not halt the troops' advance, but the fear and worry of coalition leaders could.

The sandstorm subsided on March 27, and the coalition returned to the skies with the heaviest bombing since the second night of the war. Two days later, the fog of self-doubt lifted, too. President Bush convened a meeting of his national security advisors and ordered the drive to Baghdad to continue at all costs. The Fedayeen would be dealt with as best as possible, but they would not be allowed to distract from the main effort.

It was a turning point in the war. Bush's decision to ignore the criticism from military analysts and news media was a severe psychological blow to the members of the Iraqi resistance, who saw their last ray of hope fade away. The pace of their collapse accelerated. At the same time, the president's confidence in the coalition war plan energized his own army. "Speed, speed, speed" became its watchword once again, as one marine put it. According to one military analyst, the subsequent rush of movement during the first days of April "was truly remarkable" and destined to be included among the great marches in American military history.

A Coordinated Effort

This rush was the second pulse, the race through the "red zone" that ringed Baghdad, where coalition troops were in range of chemical-filled artillery shells and rockets. The coalition assault force numbered 40,000. Opposite it was the Republican Guard, the elite of Saddam's tank force, thought to include as many as 80,000 dedicated soldiers.

Although the Republican Guard ultimately melted away before the coalition, there were several sharp engagements. At Al Kut on the Tigris, marines mowed down a "human wave" of 15 suicidal Iraqis from the Republican Guard's Baghdad Division. Other marines met resistance around Diwaniyah, between the Tigris and Euphrates, where a day-long fight cost 75 Iraqis their lives. Near Karbala on the Euphrates, troops from the 3rd Infantry Division soundly defeated the Republican Guard's Medina Division. A few days later, farther up the road to the capital, the 3rd Division faced another stiff fight. As one soldier in the division said, near Baghdad's Saddam International Airport "four hundred Iraqis made a very bad choice."

U.S. Army tanks and armored vehicles cross runways at the Baghdad airport.

Directors of the Coalition Operation Center coordinate the flying schedule.

According to Walter Rodgers, a CNN reporter traveling with the 3rd Division, the Iraqis ambushed the Americans with everything from tanks to dump trucks to pickup trucks. In all during the second pulse, fewer than 10 U.S. soldiers lost their lives.

Ultimately, it was the air war that broke down the Republican Guard. U.S. and coalition airpower had grown immeasurably since the first war with Iraq. Information pinpointing enemy targets that had taken several hours to reach pilots in 1991 took just minutes in 2003. The reason was more and better satellites, with nearly 100 in use this time around. Satellites provided coalition commanders with the location of every U.S. and British aircraft over Iraq. When an enemy target was located, the exact coordinates were beamed instantly to the coalition jet best positioned to take the shot. One of the best examples of how quickly this process could unfold was the second attempt to kill Saddam Hussein, which took place on April 7, after the major battles with the Republican Guard. Through phone calls intercepted by an eavesdropping satellite, a team of CIA and U.S. Army Delta Force commandos learned Saddam was attending a meeting at a suburban Baghdad restaurant. From the moment the attack was authorized by American officials to the time a U.S. Air Force B-1 bomber obliterated the building with four satellite-guided "bunker buster" bombs, only 15 minutes had passed.

Most often, targeting was done by radar systems like the Joint Surveillance Target Attack Radar System (JSTARS). JSTARS, a two-part system involving a U.S. Air Force radar plane and a mobile U.S. Army ground station, scoured hundreds of square miles at a time for targets. Coordinates were then passed to attacking air or ground forces. As one U.S. Air Force general noted, U.S. commanders "knew the layout of the Republican

"Bunker buster" bombs, like those used in the attacks on Saddam Hussein, stacked in a hangar bay

Guard forces better than their own division commanders did." The effect on Iraqi tank formations was devastating.

Another decisive edge the coalition had was the Global Positioning System (GPS), which utilized the same satellites that guided smart bombs such as bunker busters. Soldiers with GPS receivers rarely got lost, and they were able to call in air strikes or artillery fire against the enemy without bringing the barrage down on themselves. In battle, the GPS told American and British commanders the locations of the soldiers and tanks of their own units, those of nearby friendly units, and those of the enemy. This detailed knowledge allowed coalition tank formations to maneuver rapidly and effectively. Those Republican Guards not pummeled from the air—or who had not already retreated to the temporary safety of Baghdad—were shocked by the sudden appearance of coalition tanks.

A rocket takes off carrying a GPS satellite. The satellites are so accurate that time can be calculated within 25 billionths of a second, speed within a fraction of a mile per hour, and location to within 52 feet.

One of the coalition's strengths was its use of advanced military technology. Above, an operator performs a weapons-targeting check on a B-52 bomber during a bombing mission using an integrated system of onboard computers. Not all of the technology used in the war was electronic, however. K-Dog (left) was a member of a corps of U.S. military-trained bottlenose dolphins that searched for mines in the Persian Gulf.

Predictably, Information Minister al-Sahhaf foresaw doom and gloom for the coalition. "They will try to enter Baghdad," he said, "and I think this is where their graveyard will be." He flatly denied the Americans had captured Saddam International Airport, even as U.S. planes landed with troops and supplies. In one of his more colorful outbursts, al-Sahhaf assured his listeners that "the infidels" were "committing suicide by the hundreds on the gates of Baghdad" and "as our leader Saddam Hussein said, 'God is grilling their stomachs in hell.'"

Not all Iraqis were as anti-American as al-Sahhaf, however. In the midst of the second pulse on April 2, Private Jessica Lynch, captured during an ambush of the U.S. Army supply column in An Nasiriyah earlier in the war, was rescued from nearby Saddam Hospital by U.S. commandos. They had been tipped off about Lynch's whereabouts by "Mohammed," a local lawyer whose wife was a nurse at the hospital. Mohammed

News footage of former prisoner of war Jessica Lynch as she was airlifted to medical facilities following her dramatic rescue

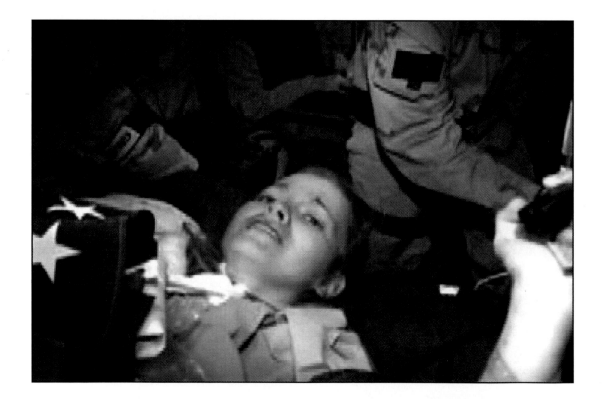

risked his life twice to help Lynch—once when he slipped out to tell nearby marines of Lynch's captivity, then again when he returned and sketched several maps of the hospital's interior. Mohammed and his family were later granted asylum in the U.S.

The Final Fights

Once past the Republican Guard, the coalition launched the final phase of the invasion, the capture of Baghdad and the overthrow of Saddam's regime. The plan had been to send raiding parties of tanks and troops into the city. They were to get in and out quickly, sizing up the enemy's defenses without being dragged into bloody street fighting. An all-out assault would follow in about a week. Franks did not want a siege, where his units would blockade the city and wait the Iraqis out. The potential for a humanitarian disaster among Baghdad's almost five million residents was too great for that. Raids, on the other hand, would show the Baathists that the coalition could move through their last stronghold at will—"a very big, deep and not so good psychological impact for the regime," according to one U.S. Army spokesman. Franks's hope was to "psych" the enemy out—to get them to quit before the fight.

It might have been wishful thinking on Franks's part to expect a surrender, since his army now faced the Special Republican Guard. Numbering about 15,000, they were Saddam's personal bodyguard, highly motivated and intensely loyal. In the end, however, with a few exceptions, this elite force crumbled like all the rest—plagued by desertions, lack of communication, and poor leadership. For example, at three key Baghdad intersections, 350 to 500 fanatical enemy soldiers died practically throwing themselves against the 3rd Infantry's tanks and armored personnel carriers. "As the fighting went on, I realized they had no organization," recalled Captain Dan Hubbard, commander of a company of M1A1 Abrams tanks. "It was like fighting a bunch of different groups that didn't know what each other were doing."

The fighters Hubbard's men engaged, an odd collection of Fedayeen, Special Republican Guard, and Syrian "volunteers," had heart, but they had no effective or even obvious leadership. It was a situation repeated throughout Baghdad—when the Iraqis stood and fought at all. Thanks to detailed maps of Baghdad drawn up by the U.S. Air Force before the war, air and ground attacks were precisely coordinated and devastatingly effective. Some of the Republican Guard tanks offered battle, and sharp firefights between dismounted forces continued sporadically for days, but there was none of the coordinated urban defense that coalition soldiers had spent months preparing for. In fact, according to an observer from the Israeli Army, the Iraqis' defense of their capital was "abysmal"—"no trenches, no barricades, no sniper positions, no booby traps, no mines." After just three days of raids, the coalition took control of the city.

In addition to Baghdad, several other key Iraqi cities fell during the final pulse, including the northern towns of Mosul, Kirkuk, and Tikrit. After weeks of intense bombing, Mosul and Kirkuk were easily seized by Kurdish Peshmerga fighters backed by coalition forces— Kirkuk on April 10 and Mosul the next day. The last major city to fall under coalition control was Tikrit, hometown to Saddam Hussein and many of the senior leaders in his regime. Iraqi forces in the area offered little resistance, and the city was overtaken on April 14.

Most of the fighting throughout Iraq had ceased by the third week of April, and President Bush declared an end to major combat operations on May 1. Coalition troops had already begun the transition from combat operations to "stability" operations—the peacekeeping and nation-building element of Operation Iraqi Freedom. In all, 173 coalition soldiers died in the military campaign, 140 Americans and 33 Britons. Almost 500 U.S. soldiers were wounded. The number of Iraqi military dead was estimated at around 3,200 soldiers, and about 13,800 more were captured or surrendered. Even more, perhaps as many as 400,000, in fact, seemed to have simply given up and fled.

Haidar Hatan Khthair, an Iraqi soldier who quit after a particularly nasty attack by U.S. warplanes, described his battered unit as "devastated" and "ruined psychologically." "I saw officers ripping off their epaulettes [their rank insignia] and throwing down their arms," he said. "They have no spirit to fight."

A real mystery in the weeks immediately following the military campaign was the whereabouts of Saddam Hussein and his top lieutenants. Saddam had not yet been found. Some Baath Party leaders eventually surrendered or were arrested after coalition commanders issued decks of playing cards to their troops emblazoned with the faces of the wanted Iraqis. Catching some of these leaders, who had brutalized their people for decades, helped convince Iraqis that they could finally leave the terror of the old Iraq behind and start building the new.

General Tommy Franks, commander of coalition forces in the war, strides through the rubble of one of Saddam Hussein's palaces destroyed by a Tomahawk missile.

AFTERWORD

Building a Free Iraq

Operation Iraqi Freedom did not end with the fall of Saddam Hussein. Although Saddam no longer ruled, the coalition needed to secure Iraq and begin the process of rebuilding the country's infrastructure and institutions.

Coalition troops remained in Iraq after the combat ended, using military force to prevent lawlessness. It was frustrating work. In the first weeks, many Iraqis engaged in widespread looting and destruction; government offices, hospitals, warehouses, oil-production facilities, and schools were robbed of anything people could haul away. Thieves even stole dozens of valuable artifacts from Baghdad's National Museum. It was also dangerous and often deadly work. In the six months after President Bush declared the end of major combat operations, more than 200 U.S. soldiers lost their lives.

In addition to subduing unrest, coalition soldiers continued to comb Iraq for weapons of mass destruction. In the months following the fighting, success was elusive. Even after visiting most of the likely hiding places around Baghdad, the coalition found no convincing proof that Iraq retained stocks of chemical and biological weapons, or that Saddam had been trying to build a nuclear bomb. David Kay, chief U.S. weapons inspector, testified before Congress on October 2 that "deliberate dispersal and destruction of material and documentation related to weapons programs" by members of Saddam's Baath Party began before the war and continued during the looting that followed. Their success at destroying the evidence may keep the world

Coalition soldiers took part in a variety of reconstruction projects in Iraq after combat ended. At left, U.S. Navy steelworkers and electricians clean the area outside the An Nasiriyah police headquarters, which was damaged by warfare and looting.

from ever knowing the whole truth about Iraq's weapons program. Iraqi scientists and former government officials said that Iraq destroyed its weapons of mass destruction during the 1990s and was only making conventional weapons. They acknowledged documents about weapons were destroyed.

After May 1, many fugitives from Saddam's regime were captured by the coalition. U.S. soldiers patrolling cities and towns received hundreds of tips from local residents, many glad to turn in former government officials. One tipster revealed the whereabouts of Saddam's two sons, Uday and Qusay, who were hiding in a house in Mosul, a city in northern Iraq. On July 22, the two men resisted capture by U.S. troops and were killed in the gunfight that followed. Qusay's teenage son, Mustapha, and a bodyguard were also killed. Intelligence sources also helped capture fugitives. On December 13, U.S. soldiers used information gathered during the interrogation of Saddam's closest associates to locate and capture the Iraqi dictator, who was hiding near his hometown of Tikrit.

The coalition also searched for terrorists and evidence of terrorism. Troops had already discovered several training camps. One, at Salman Pak near Baghdad, included an old airliner presumably for teaching aircraft hijacking. Another, in northern Iraq, belonged to Ansar Al Islam, a terrorist organization reputedly linked to Osama bin Laden's al-Qaeda. On April 14, U.S. Special Forces commandos captured Palestinian terrorist Abu Abbas in Baghdad. Abbas masterminded the 1985 hijacking of the Italian cruise ship *Achille Lauro*, during which American passenger Leon Klinghoffer was killed.

Another of the coalition's major concerns was delivering humanitarian aid to the Iraqi people. Before the invasion, six of every ten Iraqis had depended on the government's oil-for-food program for all their food. After the upheaval of the war, even more citizens needed assistance. The U.S. Agency for International Development (USAID) provided more than 500,000 tons of food to feed the people of Iraq. It also gave

U.S. soldiers examine the hole in the ground where Saddam was found hiding. Called a "spider hole," the dictator's hiding space was little more than a tiny dirt cubicle with a trap door.

almost $500 million to relief organizations operating in Iraq, such as the Red Cross, UNICEF, and the UN. These organizations struggled to do their job, however, amid the continuing violence. UN headquarters in Baghdad was bombed on August 19, killing 22 people, including the UN's chief representative, and wounding 150. Suicide bombers attacked the Red Cross building on October 27, killing at least 10 people.

USAID also awarded multimillion-dollar contracts to companies that would help to rebuild Iraq. The coalition needed to repair Iraq's damaged infrastructure, restoring services such as law enforcement and garbage collection; utilities such as water, electricity, sewage, telephone, and public transportation; and institutions such as schools, prisons, hospitals, and post offices. According to USAID, Iraq's infrastructure had suffered far less from coalition bombing (which tried not to destroy necessary services) than from years of neglect by Saddam Hussein, who spent public funds on weapons and his own lavish lifestyle. But the needs of the Iraqi people were greater than the Bush administration had anticipated. Iraqis suffered through the long, hot summer of 2003 with frequent power outages or lack of water. Many months after the war ended, oil production remained at a fraction of what it had been before the conflict.

The cost of reconstruction and peacekeeping was also higher than the U.S. government had estimated. In September, Bush asked Congress for an additional $20 billion to rebuild Iraq. In October, 70 countries met in Madrid, Spain, to discuss the reconstruction of Iraq. UN Secretary-General Kofi Annan asked the participants to "give and give generously." Eventually, however, Iraq itself would have to provide its people with food, jobs, and services. The Bush administration planned to help remake the Iraqi economy as a free-market system, in which (as in the United States) companies were owned by individuals and operated with little or no interference from the government. On May 22, the UN Security Council aided the new economy by voting to end the sanctions that had restricted Iraq's trade for the last 13 years, allowing the country to begin exporting oil once again.

The coalition's final objective was to establish a democratic government in Iraq. To accomplish this, it needed to keep all of the nation's various ethnic, religious, and political groups together, despite their widely divergent beliefs and goals. None could dominate, and none could be allowed to declare independence and form its own nation. On July 13, a 25-member Iraqi Governing Council was formed with representatives from all the major groups. In a resolution passed three months later, the UN Security Council stated this council "embodies the sovereignty of the State of Iraq during the transitional period." This resolution also recognized the coalition's authority to exercise power, but called for the coalition to restore the responsibility of governing Iraq to the Iraqi people "as soon as practicable."

Helping to form a stable government in which all could participate was one of the most important contributions the coalition could make toward peace in Iraq and the Middle East. The process might be a long and difficult one, for centuries of strife could not be resolved immediately. But with the removal of a violent dictator, the first steps had been taken. "We'll get [Iraqis] off on the right start and then they'll be in control of their own lives," said Jay Garner, head of the U.S. Office for Reconstruction and Humanitarian Assistance during the war. "This country has great vibrancy to it. It has an educated population that was the jewel of the Middle East at one time and it can be the jewel of the Middle East again."

One of the goals of reconstruction was to make sure the Iraqi people had food and water available to them. Here, U.S. Army Lt. Col. Randy Stagner gives two Iraqis a "Humanitarian Daily Ration" meal.

Timeline

1921
Iraq is created; King Faisal I is installed as leader by the British

1927
Oil is discovered in Iraq

1932
October 3: Iraq becomes an independent state

1937
April 28: Saddam Hussein is born

1948
May: The state of Israel is created

1958
July 14: Iraq's monarchy is overthrown in a military coup led by Abdul Karim Qasim and Abdul al-Salam Muhammad Arif. Iraq is declared a republic and Qasim becomes prime minister.

1963
Qasim is assassinated and Arif takes over (his brother succeeds him in 1966)

1968
July 17: A Baath-led coup ousts Abdul al-Rahman Muhammad Arif. Ahmad Hassan al-Bakr becomes president. Saddam Hussein is appointed head of security and later becomes vice president.

1979

January 16: The Islamic Revolution deposes the Shah of Iran; Ayatollah Khomeini returns to Iran to rule the country

July 16: Saddam Hussein becomes president, replacing al-Bakr

1980

September: Iraq attacks Iran, beginning an eight-year war

1988

February-September: Iraq uses chemical weapons, mass executions, and forced relocation to terrorize the Kurds in northern Iraq, resulting in about 100,000 deaths

August 20: The Iran-Iraq War ends in stalemate; no territory changes hands, and an estimated one million soldiers are killed

1990

August 2: Iraq invades Kuwait

August 6: UN Resolution 661 imposes economic sanctions on Iraq

August 7: The first U.S. forces arrive in Kuwait; Operation Desert Shield begins

November 29: UN Resolution 678 gives Iraq until January 15, 1991, to leave Kuwait or face war with a U.S.-led coalition

1991

January 15: The deadline for Resolution 678 passes

January 17: Operation Desert Storm and the air war begin

January 27: Coalition air supremacy is declared

February 24: The ground war begins

February 26: Iraq begins to retreat; U.S. Marines retake the U.S. embassy in Kuwait

February 27-28: Coalition forces control Kuwait; hostilities end

March 1: Cease-fire terms are negotiated

1991 continued

March-April: The Iraqi military suppresses rebellions in northern and southern Iraq, killing Kurds and Shi'ah. Through Operation Provide Comfort, the coalition establishes a no-fly zone in northern Iraq to protect the Kurds.

April 3: UN Resolution 687 requires Iraq to end its weapons of mass destruction programs and maintains economic sanctions

April 5: UN Resolution 688 orders Iraq to stop repressing its people

April 6: Iraq officially accepts the cease-fire terms

August 15: UN Resolution 706 authorizes Iraq to sell oil to buy food; Iraq does not accept

1992

August: The coalition establishes a no-fly zone in southern Iraq (Operation Southern Watch)

1995

April 14: UN Resolution 986 offers Iraq another opportunity to sell oil to buy food

1996

May 20: Iraq accepts Resolution 986

August-September: Iraq invades Kurdish territory; the coalition launches cruise missiles and expands northern no-fly zone (Operation Desert Strike/Operation Northern Watch)

1998

December 16-19: The coalition launches missile strikes to punish Saddam for evicting weapons inspectors and to destroy suspected weapons facilities (Operation Desert Fox)

1999

December 17: UN Resolution 1284 erases the limit on the amount of oil Iraq can sell and eases sanctions on many imported items

2001
September 11: Al-Qaeda terrorists attack the World Trade Center and the Pentagon

2002
July: U.S. begins a military buildup against Iraq

October: U.S. Congress authorizes President George W. Bush to enforce UN resolutions regarding Iraq, with armed force if necessary

November 8: UN Resolution 1441 orders Iraq to end its banned weapons programs and participate in a new series of inspections

2003
March 17: Bush gives Saddam a 48-hour ultimatum to leave Iraq or face war

March 19: First "decapitation" strike is aimed at Iraqi leadership in Baghdad

March 20: Coalition invades Iraq

March 21: Port of Umm Qasr is secured

March 23: Bridges at An Nasiriyah are captured

April 7: Second "decapitation" strike hits restaurant where Iraqi leaders are believed to be meeting

April 9: Baghdad is captured

April 10: Kirkuk falls

April 11: Mosul falls

April 14: Saddam Hussein's hometown, Tikrit, falls

May 1: Bush declares end to major combat operations

May 22: UN Resolution 1483 ends economic sanctions against Iraq

July 13: The Iraqi Governing Council is formed

July 22: Saddam's sons, Uday and Qusay, resist capture by coalition forces and are killed

August 19: UN headquarters in Baghdad is bombed, killing 22 people and wounding 150 others

December 13: U.S. forces locate and capture Saddam Hussein outside of Tikrit

Glossary

Arabs: the ethnic majority in the Middle East

artillery: large-caliber weapons, such as cannons and missile launchers, that are operated by a crew

assassination: the murder of a well-known person by surprise attack; often done for political reasons

autocracy: a nation governed by one person with unlimited power

Baath Party: a socialist political party believing that all Arabs should unite against Israel and Western influences, active mostly in Syria and Iraq

ballistic missile: a missile that has a guided and controlled ascent, but a free-fall descent

biological weapons: weapons armed with diseases or other toxic biological products, such as cholera, botulism, typhoid, and anthrax

bunker: a protective chamber, usually underground

chemical weapons: weapons armed with poisons such as mustard gas or nerve agents

coalition: a group allied for a common cause

commando: an elite fighter trained to make quick raids and special missions into enemy territory

containment: a political strategy that limits an enemy country's aggression and expansion by responding with counterforce

coup: a sudden takeover of a nation's government

Crusades: military excursions made by Christian Europeans in the eleventh, twelfth, and thirteenth centuries in an attempt to take the city of Jerusalem and other places associated with the life of Jesus Christ from the Muslims

defect: to give up residence in, and loyalty to, one country in favor of another

democracy: a nation governed by the people

desertion: running away from military service

deterrence: a strategy of national defense wherein a country warns potential enemies that their aggression will trigger a military response, and then attacks if the aggression continues

exile: being absent or living away from one's native country, either by choice or by force

free-market economy: an economy where companies are owned by individuals and operated with little or no government interference. The United States is an example of a free-market economy.

friendly fire: the firing of a weapon that injures or kills an ally

Global Positioning System (GPS): a system of satellites and portable receivers that enable a user to determine his or her exact location

guerrilla: a member of an irregular, usually independent, military group that attacks the enemy in occupied territory

imminent threat: danger that appears unavoidable and about to occur

infrastructure: the basic services and facilities needed for the functioning of a community, such as electricity, hospitals, and communication systems

interrogation: the process of formally questioning someone

Islam: a religion that views Muhammad as the primary and last prophet of God; the predominant religion of the Middle East

Kurds: Iraq's largest ethnic minority

Middle East: the area where Europe, Asia, and Africa meet

monarchy: a nation that is ruled by a sole individual, such as a king or an emperor, who inherits the position for life

Muslim: a believer in Islam

nerve agent: a poison chemical, such as sarin or VX, that interferes with the functioning of the nervous system

no-fly zone: airspace in which certain aircraft are not allowed to fly

nuclear weapon: a bomb that causes an explosion by means of a nuclear reaction (something that causes a change in an atomic nucleus)

Ottoman Empire: the empire that controlled Turkey and much of the Middle East from 1453 to 1916

police state: a country in which the government strictly controls the behavior of its people, especially by a secret, often violent, police force

rogue nation: a country that operates aggressively outside of international law

sanctions: penalties imposed on countries for violating international law

Shi'ah (also known as Shi'ite): a branch of Islam; its followers are a minority in most of the Middle East but a majority in Iraq

sortie: a flight of one or more combat aircraft on a mission

Sunni: the branch of Islam followed by the majority of Muslims

terrorism: the illegal use of violence or threats in an attempt to force people and governments to behave in a certain way

theocracy: a nation governed by religious authority

weapons of mass destruction: chemical, biological, and nuclear weapons that can kill large numbers of people in a single attack

Bibliography

Books

Cockburn, Andrew, and Patrick Cockburn. *Out of the Ashes: The Resurrection of Saddam Hussein*. New York: HarperCollins, 1999.

Cohen, Warren I. *The Cambridge History of Foreign Relations Volume IV: America in the Age of Soviet Power, 1945-1991*. New York: Cambridge University, 1995.

Coughlin, Con. *Saddam: King of Terror*. New York: HarperCollins, 2002.

Paterson, Thomas G. *American Foreign Relations Since 1895*. Lexington, Mass.: D. C. Heath, 1995.

Pollack, Kenneth M. *Arabs at War: Military Effectiveness, 1948-1991*. Lincoln: University of Nebraska, 2002.

————. *The Threatening Storm: The Case for Invading Iraq*. New York: Random House, 2002.

Woodward, Bob. *The Commanders*. New York: Simon & Schuster, 1991.

News Articles

Andrews, Mark. "War with Iraq Means Faster, Better Weapons." *Orlando Sentinel*, March 20, 2003.

Becker, Elizabeth. "U.S. Is Assembling a Civilian Team to Run Iraq." *New York Times*, March 25, 2003.

Black, Eric. "24 Years of Saddam." *Minneapolis Star-Tribune*, February 16, 2003.

Branigin, William. "3 Key Battles Turned Tide of Invasion." *Washington Post*, April 20, 2003.

Brinkley, C. Mark. "Terror Training Camp Seized, U.S. Says." *USA Today*, April 6, 2003.

Broder, John M. "Franks Describes a War 'Unlike Any Other' in History." *New York Times*, March 23, 2003.

Bumiller, Elisabeth. "Aides Say Bush Girds for War in Solitude, But Not in Doubt." *New York Times*, March 8, 2003.

Burns, John F. "U.S. Airstrikes Hit Key Targets in Iraqi Capital." *New York Times*, March 21, 2003.

Dwyer, Jim. "2 Apaches Are Down, 30 Others Retreat." *New York Times*, March 24, 2003.

Easterbrook, Gregg A. "JDAM the Torpedoes: The Weapons and Tactics We Will Use in Iraq." *Slate*, March 5, 2003.

Elliott, Michael. "Getting Iraq Wrong." *Time*, October 6, 2003.

Filkins, Dexter. "As Many Iraqis Give Up, Some Fiercely Resist." *New York Times*, March 23, 2003.

Fisher, Ian. "Displaying Solidarity, Many Iraqis Go Home." *New York Times*, March 26, 2003.

————. "Iraqi Says He Stalks and Kills Baath Party Men, with Toll at 12." *New York Times*, April 28, 2003.

Garamone, Jim. "Press and Military Seem to Appreciate Media Embeds." American Forces Press Service, March 26, 2003.

Gordon, Michael R. "The Fog of Peace." *New York Times*, May 1, 2003.

Hafidh, Hassan. "Looters Ransack Baghdad's Antiquities Museum." *Washington Post*, April 12, 2003.

Halperin, Morton H. "A Case for Containment." *Washington Post*, February 11, 2003.

Hamza, Khidhir. "Inside Iraq's Secret Nuclear Program." *Bulletin of the Atomic Scientists*, September/October 1998.

Kelly, Jack. "Doctors Might Be Treating Saddam in Bunker." *USA Today*, March 24, 2003.

Kelly, Michael. "A Chronology of Defiance." *Washington Post*, September 18, 2002.

Kifner, John. "Weather Impedes Coalition Even More Than Iraqi Resistance." *New York Times*, March 25, 2003.

King, Neil, Jr. "Bush Officials Draft Broad Plan For Free-Market Economy in Iraq." *Wall Street Journal*, May 1, 2003.

Leventhal, Paul, and Steven Dolley. "Iraq's Inspector Games." *Washington Post*, November 29, 1998.

Lippman, Thomas W., and Peter Baker. "U.S. Begins 'Shock and Awe' Campaign." *Washington Post*, March 21, 2003.

Lippman, Thomas W., and Terry M. Neal. "Aerial Assault of Baghdad Continues as Ground Forces Move into Southern Iraq." *Washington Post*, March 20, 2003.

Lippman, Thomas W., Terry M. Neal, and Alan Sipress. "Fighting Intensifies on Urban Landscape." *Washington Post*, April 8, 2003.

Macartney, Jane. "Afghanistan Offers U.S. Lessons for Rebuilding Iraq." Reuters News Service, March 12, 2003.

McFarling, Usha Lee. "The Eyes and Ears of War." *Los Angeles Times*, April 24, 2003.

McGeary, Johanna. "Looking Beyond Saddam." *Time*, March 10, 2003.

El-Magd, Nadia Abou. "Arab World Erupts in Fury Over Iraq Attack." *Washington Post*, March 20, 2003.

Moniz, Dave. "U.S. Prepares Troops to Resist Chemical Attacks." *USA Today*, February 11, 2003.

Nichols, Bill. "Republican Guard's Fiercest Division Blocks Way to Baghdad." *USA Today*, March 25, 2003.

———. "U.S. Under Pressure to Find Banned Weapons." *USA Today*, March 24, 2003.

Press, Daryl G. "The Myth of Air Power in the Persian Gulf War and the Future of Warfare." *International Security*, Fall 2001.

Priest, Dana. "U.S. Teams Seek to Kill Iraqi Elite." *Washington Post*, March 29, 2003.

Raspberry, William. "Our Insane Focus on Iraq." *Washington Post*, September 9, 2002.

Record, Jeffrey. "The Bush Doctrine and War with Iraq." *Parameters*, Spring 2003.

"Republican Guard Heads Toward U.S. Troops." *USA Today*, March 26, 2003.

Ricks, Thomas E. "U.S. Losses Expose Risks, Raise Doubts About Strategy." *Washington Post*, March 24, 2003.

———. "What Counted: People, Plan, Inept Enemy." *Washington Post*, April 10, 2003.

Sanger, David E. "A Stalwart of Certainty: Bush Undeterred on Iraq." *New York Times*, March 2, 2003.

Shadid, Anthony. "Iraqis Now Feel Free to Disagree." *Washington Post*, April 10, 2003.

Sheridan, Mary Beth. "U.S. Apache Helicopter Downed in Iraqi-Held Territory." *Washington Post*, March 24, 2003.

Shultz, George P. "Act Now." *Washington Post*, September 6, 2002.

Smith, Craig S. "Iraqis Tell of a Reign of Torture and Maiming." *New York Times*, April 23, 2003.

"Troops Find Terror Training Camp in Iraq." *New York Times*, April 16, 2003.

Tyler, Patrick E. "U.S. Helicopters Turned Back in Clash With Republican Guard." *New York Times*, March 21, 2003.

Walsh, Edward. "U.S. Sketches Plan for Postwar 'Iraqi Interim Authority.'" *Washington Post*, March 15, 2003.

Walt, Vivienne. "Special Operations Forces Fight for Strategic Bases." *USA Today*, March 25, 2003.

Walt, Vivienne, and Paul Wiseman. "U.S. Closes in on Fugitives From Many Angles." *USA Today*, April 27, 2003.

Williams, Daniel. "Rampant Looting Sweeps Iraq." *Washington Post*, April 12, 2003.

Web Articles and Websites

Brahimi, Rym, et al. "U.S., Coalition Troops Push Into Iraq." CNN.com, March 20, 2003.

————. "U.S.: Strikes Pave Way for Full-Fledged Attack." CNN.com, March 20, 2003.

Ensor, David. "Al-Qaeda-tied Terrorist Nabbed in Iraq." CNN.com, April 29, 2003.

Global Security. www. globalsecurity.org.

"Mohammed Saeed al-Sahhaf, Face of Iraqi Government." CNN.com, April 8, 2003.

"'Sharpest' Fighting in War to Date." CNN.com, March 24, 2003.

"Text of Iraq Weapons Inspector David Kay's Congressional Testimony." http://www.sign onsandiego.com/news/world/iraq/20031002-1830-kay-text.html, October 2, 2003.

United Nations. www.un.org.

U.S. Agency for International Development. www.usaid.gov.

U.S. Department of Defense. www.dod.gov.

U.S. Department of State International Information Programs. www.usinfo.state.gov.

The White House. www.whitehouse.org.

Index

typhoid, 17

Umm Qasr, 72-73, 74, 77
UNICEF, 93
United Nations (UN), 30, 43, 52, 66, 93;
    inspectors in Iraq, 7, 42, 44, 45-47, 49,
    52, 60, 62, 67; resolutions of, 27, 41,
    42, 59, 60; Security Council of, 7, 27, 41,
    43, 49, 51, 59, 62, 94
United States: Bush Doctrine as policy of,
    56-57, 59, 60-61; containment policy
    of, 41-43, 49, 52, 53; and creation of
    Israel, 12-13; deterrence policy of, 55-
    56; interests of, in Middle East, 12, 16,
    18, 21, 25, 66; as leader of Operation
    Iraqi Freedom coalition, 5, 7, 69, 71,
    72-76, 77, 78, 80, 81-85, 88, 94; in
    Persian Gulf War coalition, 27, 28, 31,
    32-33, 35, 39, 41, 42, 52; reaction of, to
    September 11 attacks, 7, 55-56, 60;
    support of Iraq by, 20-21, 26
UN Monitoring, Verification, and Inspection
    Committee (UNMOVIC), 62
uranium, 47
U.S. Agency for International Development
    (USAID), 92-93
U.S. Office for Reconstruction and
    Humanitarian Assistance, 95

VX (nerve agent), 17, 28, 45

Washington Post, 47, 61
weapons of mass destruction, 56, 57, 91-
    92; developed by Saddam Hussein, 7,
17, 21-22, 25, 41-42, 45-47, 52, 58, 69;
not found after Operation Iraqi
Freedom, 91-92; search for, by UN
inspectors, 7, 17-18, 42, 44, 45-47
Webster, Daniel, 60
Wisconsin, USS, 31
World Trade Center, 55, 56
World War I, 5, 10
World War II, 9, 12, 55

About the Author

Jason Richie is the author of several titles from The Oliver Press, including *Secretaries of State: Making Foreign Policy*; *Secretaries of War, Navy, and Defense: Ensuring National Security*; *Space Flight: Crossing the Last Frontier*; *Spectacular Space Travelers*; and *Weapons: Designing the Tools of War*. A former noncommissioned officer in the U.S. Army, Richie graduated summa cum laude from the University of Minnesota with a degree in American history. He lives in Houston, Texas, with his wife, Diana, and son, James.

Photo Credits